First World War
and Army of Occupation
War Diary
France, Belgium and Germany

66 DIVISION
199 Infantry Brigade,
Brigade Trench Mortar Battery
1 August 1917 - 28 February 1918

WO95/3145/8

The Naval & Military Press Ltd
www.nmarchive.com
Published in association with The National Archives

Published by

The Naval & Military Press Ltd

Unit 10 Ridgewood Industrial Park,

Uckfield, East Sussex,

TN22 5QE England

Tel: +44 (0) 1825 749494

www.naval-military-press.com

www.nmarchive.com

This diary has been reprinted in facsimile from the original. Any imperfections are inevitably reproduced and the quality may fall short of modern type and cartographic standards.

© Crown Copyright
Images reproduced by permission of The National Archives, London, England, 2015.

Contents

Document type	Place/Title	Date From	Date To
Heading	WO95/3145/8 Brigade Trench Mortar Battery		
Heading	66th Division 199th Infy Bde Trench Mortar Battery Aug 1917-Feb 1918		
Heading	War Diary of 199th L.T.M.B From Aug 1st-1917 To Aug 31st 1917 (Volume I)		
War Diary	Lombartzyde Sector	01/08/1917	03/08/1917
War Diary	Coxyde Bains	04/08/1917	10/08/1917
War Diary	Oost Dunkirk	11/08/1917	20/08/1917
War Diary	Coxyde Bains (Wiltshin Camp)	22/08/1917	31/08/1917
Miscellaneous	Daily Intelligence Summary From 6 a.m. 21.7.17 to 6 a.m. 21.8.17	31/07/1917	31/07/1917
Miscellaneous	Daily Intelligence Summary From 6 a.m. 1.8.17 to 6 a.m. 2.8.17	01/08/1917	01/08/1917
Miscellaneous	Daily Intelligence Summary From 6 a.m. 2.8.17 to 6 a.m. 3.8.17	02/08/1917	02/08/1917
Miscellaneous	Daily Intelligence Summary From 6 a.m. 10.8.17 to 6 a.m. 11.8.17	10/08/1917	10/08/1917
Miscellaneous	Daily Intelligence Summary From 6 a.m. 11.8.17 to 6 a.m. 12.8.17	11/08/1917	11/08/1917
Miscellaneous	Daily Intelligence Summary From 6 a.m. 12.8.17 to 6 a.m. 13.8.17	12/08/1917	12/08/1917
Miscellaneous	Daily Intelligence Summary From 6 a.m. 13.8.17 to 6 a.m. 14.8.17	13/08/1917	13/08/1917
Miscellaneous	Daily Intelligence Summary From 6 a.m. 14.8.17 to 6 a.m. 15.8.17	14/08/1917	14/08/1917
Miscellaneous	Daily Intelligence Summary From 6 a.m. 15.8.17 to 6 a.m. 16.8.17	15/08/1917	15/08/1917
Miscellaneous	Daily Intelligence Summary From 6 a.m. 16.8.17 to 6 a.m. 17.8.17	16/08/1917	16/08/1917
Miscellaneous	Daily Intelligence Summary From 6 a.m. 17.8.17 to 6 a.m. 18.8.17	17/08/1917	17/08/1917
Miscellaneous	Daily Intelligence Summary From 6 a.m. 18.8.17 to 6 a.m. 19.8.17	18/08/1917	18/08/1917
Miscellaneous	Daily Intelligence Summary From 6 a.m. 19.8.17 to 6 a.m. 20.8.17	19/08/1917	19/08/1917
Miscellaneous	Daily Intelligence Summary From 6 a.m. 20.8.17 to 6 a.m. 21.8.17	20/08/1917	20/08/1917
Map	Map		
War Diary	Coxyde-Bains	01/09/1917	18/09/1917
War Diary	Nieuport Bains (Surrey Camp)	19/09/1917	24/09/1917
War Diary	Coxyde Bains	25/09/1917	25/09/1917
War Diary	Ghyvelde	26/09/1917	28/09/1917
War Diary	Heurengen	29/09/1917	30/09/1917
Heading	War Diary of 199th L.T.M.B From 1st Oct-31st Oct 1917 Volume III		
War Diary	Heurenghen	01/10/1917	02/10/1917
War Diary	Brandhoek	03/10/1917	06/10/1917
War Diary	(Ypres) Zonnebeke	01/10/1917	09/10/1917
War Diary	Brandhoek (Toronto Camp)	10/10/1917	13/10/1917
War Diary	Rue Malhove Arques	14/10/1917	19/10/1917

War Diary	Campagne	20/10/1917	25/10/1917
War Diary	Rue Malhove Arques	26/10/1917	31/10/1917
Miscellaneous	Daily Intelligence Summary		
Operation(al) Order(s)	Administration Order No. 22	01/10/1917	01/10/1917
Miscellaneous	Ref. 199 Inf Bde Order No. 58	01/10/1917	01/10/1917
Miscellaneous	Correction To 199th Brigade Order No. 58	01/10/1917	01/10/1917
Miscellaneous	Addendum To 199th Infantry Brigade Operation Order No. 58	02/10/1917	02/10/1917
Miscellaneous	Addendum To Operation Order No. 58	02/10/1917	02/10/1917
Operation(al) Order(s)	199th Infantry Brigade Order No. 58	01/10/1917	01/10/1917
Miscellaneous	March Table To Accompany 199th Infantry Brigade Order No. 58		
Miscellaneous	A Form Messages And Signals.		
Operation(al) Order(s)	199 Inf. Bde Order No. 59	04/09/1917	04/09/1917
Miscellaneous	OC. 2/6th Manch. Regt	04/10/1917	04/10/1917
Miscellaneous	A Form Messages And Signals.		
Miscellaneous	OC 199th L.T.M.B	12/10/1917	12/10/1917
Miscellaneous	Warning Order	12/10/1917	12/10/1917
Operation(al) Order(s)	199 Bde Order No. 60		
Operation(al) Order(s)	199th Infantry Brigade Order No. 61	12/10/1917	12/10/1917
Miscellaneous	O.C., 2/5th Bn Manchester Regt.	19/10/1917	19/10/1917
Miscellaneous	199th Infantry Brigade Movement Order	24/10/1917	24/10/1917
Operation(al) Order(s)	199th Infantry Brigade Order No. 62	28/10/1917	28/10/1917
Miscellaneous	Diagram Of Inspection And March Past		
Operation(al) Order(s)	199th Infantry Brigade Order No. 63	30/10/1917	30/10/1917
Diagram etc	Diagram To Accompany 199 Bde Order No. 63		
Miscellaneous	Warning Order		
Miscellaneous	Copy A.F.W. 5210 Service in France 7/12		
War Diary	Wallon Cappel	01/11/1917	01/11/1917
Heading	War Diary of 199th L.T.M. Bty From 1st Nov-30th Nov 1917 Volume V		
War Diary	Arques	01/11/1917	01/11/1917
War Diary	Staple	02/11/1917	09/11/1917
War Diary	Westoutre Area	10/11/1917	10/11/1917
War Diary	Canal Area Ypres	11/11/1917	19/11/1917
War Diary	Esplanade Sap Ypres	20/11/1917	21/11/1917
War Diary	Montreal Camp Ouderdom	22/11/1917	23/11/1917
War Diary	Berthen Area	24/11/1917	25/11/1917
War Diary	Staple Sub-Area No 2 (Eastern)	26/11/1917	30/11/1917
Miscellaneous	Appendix		
Operation(al) Order(s)	199th Infantry Brigade Order No. 64	31/10/1917	31/10/1917
Miscellaneous	March Table To Accompany 199th Infantry Brigade Order No. 64		
Miscellaneous	199th Infantry Brigade Administrative Order No. 23	31/10/1917	31/10/1917
Miscellaneous	Administrative Order No. 24	07/11/1917	07/11/1917
Miscellaneous	Addendum To Administrative Order No. 24	08/11/1917	08/11/1917
Miscellaneous	Administrative Order No. 25	08/11/1917	08/11/1917
Miscellaneous	Administrative Order No. 26	09/11/1917	09/11/1917
Miscellaneous	Addendum To 199th Infantry Brigade Order No. 67	18/11/1917	18/11/1917
Miscellaneous	Addendum To 199th Infantry Brigade Order No. 68	21/11/1917	21/11/1917
Miscellaneous	Administrative Order No. 30	22/11/1917	22/11/1917
Miscellaneous	Addendum To 199th Infantry Brigade Administrative Order No. 30	23/11/1917	23/11/1917
Miscellaneous	199th Infantry Brigade Administrative Order No. 31		
Miscellaneous	199th Infantry Brigade Administrative Order No. 32	25/11/1917	25/11/1917

Miscellaneous	Addendum To 199th Infantry Brigade Administrative Order No. 32	25/11/1917	25/11/1917
Miscellaneous	Warning Order No. 2	06/11/1917	06/11/1917
Operation(al) Order(s)	199th Infantry Brigade Order No. 65	08/11/1917	08/11/1917
Miscellaneous	Move Table		
Operation(al) Order(s)	199 Inf. Bde. Order No. 66	09/11/1917	09/11/1917
Miscellaneous	March Table To Accompany 199 Inf. Bde. Order No. 66		
Miscellaneous	199th Infantry Brigade Warning Order	16/11/1917	16/11/1917
Operation(al) Order(s)	199th Infantry Brigade Order No. 67	17/11/1917	17/11/1917
Miscellaneous	Relief Table		
Operation(al) Order(s)	199th Infantry Brigade Order No. 68	22/11/1917	22/11/1917
Miscellaneous	March Table To Accompany 199th Infantry Brigade Order No. 68		
Miscellaneous	B.Casualty		
Operation(al) Order(s)	199th Infantry Brigade Order No. 69	22/11/1917	22/11/1917
Miscellaneous	March Table To Accompany 199th Infantry Brigade Order No. 69		
Miscellaneous	O.C. 204 Mg Coy	25/11/1917	25/11/1917
Operation(al) Order(s)	199th Infantry Brigade Order No. 70	25/11/1917	25/11/1917
Miscellaneous	March Table To Accompany 199th Infantry Brigade Order No. 70		
Miscellaneous	Summary Of Events For The Month		
Miscellaneous	Summary Of Events	30/11/1917	30/11/1917
Heading	War Diary of 199th L.T.M Battery From 1st Dec-31st Dec Volume V		
War Diary	St. Sylvestre Cappel (Caestre Area)	01/12/1917	31/12/1917
Miscellaneous	Warning Order 199th Infantry Brigade	14/12/1917	14/12/1917
Miscellaneous	Administrative Order No. 32	15/12/1917	15/12/1917
Operation(al) Order(s)	199th Infantry Brigade Order No. 71	15/12/1917	15/12/1917
Miscellaneous	Movement Table To Accompany 199th Inf. Bde. Order No. 71		
Miscellaneous	Administrative Order No. 33	29/12/1917	29/12/1917
Miscellaneous	Table "A"		
Miscellaneous	Table "C"		
Miscellaneous	Table "B"		
Miscellaneous	Short Summary Of Events For The Month	31/12/1917	31/12/1917
Heading	War Diary of 199th L.T.M Battery From 1st Jan-31st Jan 1918 Volume VI		
War Diary	St. Sylvestre Cappel (Caestre Area)	01/01/1918	11/01/1918
War Diary	Potijze Area	12/01/1918	12/01/1918
War Diary	Broodseinde Ridge Sector	13/01/1918	22/01/1918
War Diary	Halifax Camp	23/01/1918	27/01/1918
War Diary	Left Zonnebeke Sector	28/01/1918	31/01/1918
Miscellaneous	Daily Tactical Progress Report	12/01/1918	12/01/1918
Miscellaneous	Daily Tactical Progress Report	13/01/1918	13/01/1918
Miscellaneous	Daily Tactical Progress Report	14/01/1918	14/01/1918
Miscellaneous	Daily Tactical Progress Report	15/01/1918	15/01/1918
Miscellaneous	Daily Tactical Progress Report	16/01/1918	16/01/1918
Miscellaneous	Daily Tactical Progress Report	17/01/1918	17/01/1918
Miscellaneous	Daily Tactical Progress Report	18/01/1918	18/01/1918
Miscellaneous	Daily Tactical Progress Report	19/01/1918	19/01/1918
Miscellaneous	Daily Tactical Progress Report	20/01/1918	20/01/1918
Miscellaneous	Daily Tactical Progress Report	21/01/1918	21/01/1918
Miscellaneous	Daily Tactical Progress Report	28/01/1918	28/01/1918
Miscellaneous	Daily Tactical Progress Report	29/01/1918	29/01/1918

Type	Description	Date From	Date To
Miscellaneous	Daily Tactical Progress Report	30/01/1918	30/01/1918
Miscellaneous	199th Infantry Brigade Preliminary Order	05/01/1918	05/01/1918
Miscellaneous	March Table A.		
Operation(al) Order(s)	199th Infantry Brigade Operation Order No. 73	07/01/1918	07/01/1918
Operation(al) Order(s)	199th Infantry Brigade Operation Order No. 74	08/01/1918	08/01/1918
Miscellaneous	Movement Table-199th Infantry Brigade		
Miscellaneous	Administrative Order No. 34	08/01/1918	08/01/1918
Operation(al) Order(s)	199th Infantry Brigade Operation Order No. 75	10/01/1918	10/01/1918
Miscellaneous	Movement Table To Accompany Brigade Operation Order No 75		
Operation(al) Order(s)	199th Infantry Bde. Operation Order No. 76		
Miscellaneous	Table 'A' To Accompany 199 Brigade Operation Order No. 76		
Miscellaneous	Administrative Order No. 55	20/01/1918	20/01/1918
Operation(al) Order(s)	199th Infantry Brigade Operation Order No. 77	20/01/1918	20/01/1918
Miscellaneous	Table 'A' To Accompany 199th Infantry Brigade Order No. 77		
Operation(al) Order(s)	199th Infantry Brigade Administrative Order No. 36	26/01/1918	26/01/1918
Operation(al) Order(s)	199th Infantry Brigade Operation Order No. 78	26/01/1918	26/01/1918
Miscellaneous	Table A To Accompany 199th Infantry Brigade Order No. 78		
Miscellaneous	Table B (11) To Accompany 199th Inf. Bde. Order No. 78	28/01/1918	28/01/1918
Miscellaneous	Table B (1) To Accompany 199th Inf. Bde. Order No. 78		
Miscellaneous	Casualty Return	29/01/1918	29/01/1918
War Diary		31/01/1918	31/01/1918
Heading	War Diary of 199th L.T.M Battery From 1st Feb-28th Feb Volume VII		
War Diary	Left Zonnebeke Sector	01/02/1918	09/02/1918
War Diary	Hussar Camp	10/02/1918	10/02/1918
War Diary	Hallifax Camp	11/02/1918	11/02/1918
War Diary	School Camp	12/02/1918	17/02/1918
War Diary	Vauvillers	18/02/1918	23/02/1918
War Diary	Villers Carbonnel	24/02/1918	24/02/1918
War Diary	Vraignes	25/02/1918	25/02/1918
War Diary	R. Sub-Sector Of Villeret Sector	26/02/1918	28/02/1918
Operation(al) Order(s)	199th Infantry Brigade Operation Order No. 79	01/02/1918	01/02/1918
Operation(al) Order(s)	199th Infantry Brigade Operation Order No. 80	05/02/1918	05/02/1918
Operation(al) Order(s)	199th Infantry Brigade Administrative Order No. 37	06/02/1918	06/02/1918
Miscellaneous	Table "A"	09/02/1918	09/02/1918
Miscellaneous	Amendment To 199th Infantry Brigade Operation Order No. 80	08/02/1918	08/02/1918
Miscellaneous	Reference 199th Infantry Brigade Order No. 80	08/02/1918	08/02/1918
Miscellaneous	Table "C" (To Accompany 199th Infantry Brigade Order No. 80)	11/02/1918	11/02/1918
Miscellaneous	Reference Brigade Operation Order No. 80	10/02/1918	10/02/1918
Miscellaneous	2/5th Manchester Regt	13/02/1918	13/02/1918
Miscellaneous	Move To Fifth Army Area	14/02/1918	14/02/1918
Miscellaneous	Table A		
Miscellaneous	Table B		
Miscellaneous	199th Infantry Brigade Warning Order	20/02/1918	20/02/1918
Operation(al) Order(s)	199th Infantry Brigade Operation Order No. 81		
Miscellaneous	Table "A" To Accompany 199th Infantry Brigade Order No. 81		

Miscellaneous	Table "B" To Accompany 199th Infantry Brigade Order No. 81		
Miscellaneous	Amendment To 199th Infantry Brigade Order No. 81	28/02/1918	28/02/1918
Operation(al) Order(s)	199th Infantry Brigade Operation Order No82	23/02/1918	23/02/1918
Miscellaneous	Table "A" To Accompany 199th Infantry Brigade Order No. 82		
Miscellaneous	Administrative Order No. 38	23/02/1918	23/02/1918
Miscellaneous	Table "A" To Accompany 199th Infantry Brigade Administrative Order No. 38		
Miscellaneous	O.C. 2/5th Bn Manchester Regt.	24/02/1918	24/02/1918
Miscellaneous	War Diary		
Miscellaneous	Daily Tactical Progress Report Unit "COD" from 6 am 31.1.18 to 6 am 1.2.18		
Miscellaneous	Daily Tactical Progress Report Unit "COD" from 6 am 1.2.18 to 6 am 2.2.18		
Miscellaneous	Daily Tactical Progress Report Unit "COD" from 6 am 2.2.18 to 6 am 3.2.18		
Miscellaneous	Daily Tactical Progress Report Unit "COD" from 6 am 3.2.18 to 6 am 4.2.18		
Miscellaneous	Daily Tactical Progress Report Unit "COD" from 6 am 4.2.18 to 6 am 5.2.18		
Miscellaneous	Daily Tactical Progress Report Unit "COD" from 6 am 5.2.18 to 6 am 6.2.18		
Miscellaneous	Daily Tactical Progress Report Unit "COD" from 6 am 6.2.18 to 6 am 7.2.18		
Miscellaneous	Daily Tactical Progress Report Unit "COD" from 6 am 7.2.18 to 6 am 8.2.18		
Miscellaneous	Daily Tactical Progress Report Unit "COD" from 6 am 8.2.18 to 6 am 9.2.18		
Miscellaneous	Daily Tactical Progress Report Unit "COD" from 6 am 27.2.18 to 6 am 28.2.18		
Miscellaneous	Daily Tactical Progress Report Unit "COD" from 6 am 26.2.18 to 6 am 27.2.18		

10/25/2145/15

Brigade Trench Mortars Battery

66TH DIVISION
199TH INFY BDE

TRENCH MORTAR BATTERY
AUG 1917-FEB 1918

Army Form W.3091.

Cover for Documents.

Nature of Enclosures.

CONFIDENTIAL

War Diary
of
199th L.T.M.B.

From- Aug 1st- 1917   To- Aug 31st 1917.

(Volume I)

Notes, or Letters written.

Army Form C. 2118.

WAR DIARY
or
INTELLIGENCE SUMMARY
(Erase heading not required.)

Instructions regarding War Diaries and Intelligence Summaries are contained in F. S. Regs, Part II. and the Staff Manual respectively. Title Pages will be prepared in manuscript.

Place	Date	Hour	Summary of Events and Information	Remarks and references to Appendices
LOMBART-ZYDE. SECTOR.	Aug 1st 1917		Weather wet. O.C. 97th L.T.M.B. visited our H.Q. in NIEUPORT to arrange details to relieve the following day. Withdrew 2 Stokes guns from REDAN + two guns from SUPPORT to H.Q. NIEUPORT. 1 O.R. casualty. Rec ivd B.O.O. No: 44 Copy No: 10.	Sketch gun posn app II TPR 30/7/17 1/8/17 app II
"	Aug 2nd		Weather wet. Observations referred to in B.G.G No: 44 carried out, but the Stokes were inactive. Recvd B.O.O No: 45 Copy No: 23. Also S.g 23]. O.C. 147th L.T.M.B. arrived our H.Q. in NIEUPORT to arrange details & relieve the following day.	T.P.R. 1/8/17— 2/8/17 seq.
"	Aug 3rd		Weather wet. Recvd B.O.O No: 46 Copy No: 20. Addenda to B.O.O No 46. Relieving section of 147th L.T.M.B. arrivd NIEUPORT @ 4 P.M. Jerry artillery him active at forecast about 7 P.M. YSER. Relief complete about 7 P.M. No 1 Section + Transport left @ 7.30 P.M. N.O.H. Leaving @ 8.30 P.M. Marched via OostDuinkerk and Coxyde to COXYDE BAINS. Battery completed at COXYDE BAINS at 10.30 P.M.	T.P.R. 2/8/17— 3/8/17 seq.
COXYDE BAINS.	" 4th		Weather more settled. Nothing of importance.	seq. seq.
"	" 5th		Weather fine. Training.	seq.

2449 Wt. W14957/M90 750,000 1/16 J.B.C. & A. Forms/C.2118/12.

Army Form C. 2118

WAR DIARY
or
INTELLIGENCE SUMMARY
(Erase heading not required.)

Instructions regarding War Diaries and Intelligence Summaries are contained in F. S. Regs., Part II. and the Staff Manual respectively. Title Pages will be prepared in manuscript.

Place	Date	Hour	Summary of Events and Information	Remarks and references to Appendices
Coxyde Bains	Aug 6		Weather fine. Training.	
COXYDE BAINS.	" 7		Weather unsettled. Training. Received B.O. 48 Copy No. 9.	S.G.S.G.
	" 8		Weather unsettled. Training. Received B.O. 49 Copy No. 9. Battery instruction No. 1 Scheme "A" (66 Copies) also night Routine	S.G.
	" 9		Raw Returns. Training. O.O. 198. T.M.B. issued. H.Q. to company also. Received B.M./331.9. Agenda to O.O. No. 49 Copy No. 10. administration order No. 15 Copy No. 20.	S.G.
	" 10		Weather unsettled. B.O.O. No 50 Copy No. 10 received. Equipment Carriages W.D. to B.60 pptd. 15.O.P.s attached to Batty. The Battery refitted 198 R. Batty. Relief complete about 11.30 p.m. Left Section went into the line taking the right gun Positions on the Left sub-section – 2 Officers and 8 Other ranks. H.Q. Staff + half Section took over two huts in Middlesex Camp.	Sketch of Dispositions attached T.P.R.11/8/17 T.P.R.11/8/17 11/8/17 S.G.
"	" 11		Weather unsettled. Withdrew & however gun to the Ostercycle Road, and took two other gun out further. There fire night subsector.	T.P.R.11/8/17 12/8/17 S.G.

OOST DUNKIRK DUNKIRKE

Army Form C. 2118.

WAR DIARY
or
INTELLIGENCE SUMMARY
(Erase heading not required.)

Instructions regarding War Diaries and Intelligence Summaries are contained in F. S. Regs., Part II. and the Staff Manual respectively. Title Pages will be prepared in manuscript.

Place	Date	Hour	Summary of Events and Information	Remarks and references to Appendices
OOST	Aug 12		Weather unsettled. Our guns were active as shown in attached T.P.R.	T.P.R. 12/8/17 – 13/8/17
DUNKIRK	,, 13		Weather unsettled. Our guns were active as shown in attached T.P.R. – S.g.y.	T.P.R. 13/8/17 – 14/8/17
,,	,, 14		Weather unsettled. Our guns were active as shown in attached T.P.R. S.g.y.	T.P.R. 14/8/17 – 15/8/17
,,	,, 15		Rainy weather. Received B. Order letter 15/8/17. Usual activity by our guns.	S.g.y T.P.R. 14/8/17 – 15/8/17
,,	,, 16		Unsettled weather. Usual activity with our guns.	S.g.y T.P.R. 15/8/17 – 16/8/17
,,	,, 17		Weather fine. Received Provisional Defence Scheme Copy No. 10. Usual activity by our guns.	S.g.y T.P.R. 17/8/17 – 18/8/17
,,	,, 18		Weather fine. Received Brig. B.C. No 51 B. Copy No. 9: Also Administration Orders No 16 Copy No. 15. Usual activity by our guns. 16.R wounded. 16.R. admitted Hospital sick.	T.P.R. 18/8/17 – 19/8/17 S.g.y
,,	,, 19		Weather fine. C.C. 19th S.T.M.B called to make arrangements re relief. Usual activity by our guns.	T.P.R. 19/8/17 – 20/8/17 S.g.y
,,	,, 20		Weather fine. Usual activity by our guns.	T.P.R. 20/8/17 – 21/8/17 S.g.y

Army Form C. 2118.

WAR DIARY
or
INTELLIGENCE SUMMARY
(Erase heading not required.)

Instructions regarding War Diaries and Intelligence Summaries are contained in F. S. Regs., Part II. and the Staff Manual respectively. Title Pages will be prepared in manuscript.

Place	Date	Hour	Summary of Events and Information	Remarks and references to Appendices
CONYDE	Aug 21/15		Weather fine. No:1 Section Left H.Q. at host Quinlink Barns at 11-15 a.m. and marched to hutting camp, taking over from the 197th L.T.M.B. Gun section in the line. Guns placed at dusk. Relief complete 11.15 p.m.	S.E.9.
BAIN'S (hutting camp)	22		Weather fine. Usual training carried out. 5 O.R.s taken on strength of Battery.	S.E.9. 329
"	23		Weather unsettled. Training.	S.E.9.
"	24		Weather wet. Training	S.E.9.
"	25		Weather wet. Training	S.E.9.
"	26		Weather wet. Training. General Sug 66 no 52 & Sy/no 10. Administrative Orders no 17 & 29. & Sy no 14. Addenda & corrigenda no 7 & Sy no 14. Ap/ no 11.	S.E.9. S.E.9.
"	27		Weather wet. Training.	
"	28		Weather wet. Training.	S.E.9.
"	29		Weather wet. Training	S.E.9.
"	30		Weather wet. Training.	S.E.9.
"	31		Weather wet. Training	S.E.9.

Appendix I

Daily Intelligence Summary

Unit - "Unfrock"

From - 6.a.m. 21.7.17 to 6 a.m. 22.8.17

A. Operations.

Our guns were inactive.

B. Enemy Defences + organisation

C. Enemy Activity.

D. Information

S. C. Goodall. Lt.
for O.C.
199th L.T.M.B.

Daily Intelligence Summary

Unit — "Unfrock"

From 6 a.m. 11.8.17 to 6 a.m. 12.8.17

A Operations.

    Our guns were inactive.

B Enemy Defences + organisation

C Enemy Activity.

D Information

                                                    L.C. Goodall St:
                                                            Ao 6 B
                                                  199th L.T.M.B

Daily Intelligence Summary.

Unit — "Unfrock"

From 6.a.m 2.8.17 to 6 a.m. 3.8.17

A. Operations.
    Our guns were inactive.

B. Enemy Defences & organisation.

C. Enemy Activity.

D. Information.

                                          S.C. Goodall 2/Lt.
                                              for. O.C.
                                       199th L.T.M.B.

Daily Intelligence Summary.

Unit. Unfrock.

From 6 am. 10-8-17 to 6 am. 11-8-17.

A Information:-

Our Light Trench Mortars inactive owing to relief.

B Enemy defences & organisation

C Enemy Activity.

D Information.

S.C. Goodall Lt
for O.C.
199th LTMB

Daily Intelligence Summary.

Unit - Munrock.

From 6am 11-8-17 to 6am 12-8-17.

A Operations:

Our guns were active in ranging. At 3·45pm our four guns at M14c 90·70 fired 80 rounds on suspected enemy M.Gs and T.M. emplacements behind the barricade between M14d 60·80 & M14 B 30·40.

Our two guns at M14c 60·90 fired 40 rounds at 4 pm on enemy C.T. from M14b 10·45 to M14b 30·50, with good results.

Very slight retaliation.

B Enemy defences & organisation:

C Enemy Activity.

D Information.

S.C. Goodall Lt.
for O.C.
Munrock.

Daily Intelligence Summary.

Unit:- Unfrock.

From 6 a.m. 12.8.17 to 6 a.m. 13.8.17.

A) Operations:- Our Stokes were active in ranging at 8.30 a.m., our 4 guns at M14 c 90.70 firing 120 rounds searching fire immediately behind the barricade. At the same time our 2 guns at M14 c 60.90 fired 60 rounds on enemy C.T. from M14 b 10.45 to M14 b 30.50. Many of the shells were observed to fall right into trench causing much damage to same.

B) Enemy defences + organisation.

C) Enemy Activity.

D) Information.

S.C. Goodall, Lt.
for OC.
"Unfrock."

Daily Intelligence Summary

Unit:- Unfrock.

From 6 a.m. 13-8-17 to 6 a.m. 14-8-17

A _Operations_:- At 11.45 a.m. our 2 guns at M.20.b.95.50 and M.20.b.70.65 fired 20 ranging shots on to Back Hack at approximately M.15.d.30.20 & M.15.c.50.75 respectively. At 1.15 a.m. our 2 guns at M.14.c.80.60 and at M.14.c.60.80 fired 100 rounds on the new work apparent on Beach Avenue between M.14.b.10.45 and M.14.b.40.50 with good results. At the same time our guns at M.14.c.85.55 fired 50 rounds traversing along newly observed trench running parallel to and about 50 yds behind barricade. Good results were observed.

B _Enemy defences - organisation._

C _Enemy Activity_

D _Information_:- In consequence of our ranging shots on the right sub. sector a flight of about 100 pigeons was put up at about M.15.b.30.30.

S.C. Goodall, Lt.
for O.C.
Unfrock.

Daily Intelligence Summary.

Unit. "Unfrock"

From 6 a.m. 14.8.17 to 6. a.m. 15.8.17.

A/ Operations:- At 12.30 p.m. our 2 guns at M14c90.70 fired on to the trench which runs parallel to & about 50 yards behind the barricade, particularly concentrating on a large pile of brushwood at M14b 62.25 on which several direct hits were obtained. 100 Rounds were fired in all.

At the same time our gun at M14c 60.90 fired 50 rounds into the enemy C.T. between M14b 10.45 and M14b 30.50. He retaliated somewhat heavily with 4.2's.

B/ Enemy defences & organisation:

C/ Enemy Activity.

D/ Information

SL Goodall Lt.
for O.C.
199th L.T.M.B.

Daily Intelligence Summary

Unit: "Unfrock"

From 6 a.m. 15.8.17 to 6 a.m. 16.8.17.

A. Operations:— Our guns fired their usual programme for the day. At 2·45 p.m. our two guns at M.14.c.80.60 fired 100 rounds concentrating on apparent camouflage of brushwood at M.14.c.35.25, upwards of 10 direct hits being obtained. This brushwood was suspected of camouflaging trench running parallel to and about 50 yds behind barricade. At the same time our gun at M.14.c.60.80 fired 50 rounds on Beach Avenue between M.14.b.10.50 and M.14.b.30.60 with good results. Retaliation to this stunt was practically Nil. Our other guns were inactive.

B. Enemy defences & organisation.

C. Enemy Activity.

D. Information.

S.C. Goodall. Lt.
for O.C.
"Unfrock"

Daily Intelligence Summary

Unit. Nieuprock.

From 6 am 16.8.17 to 6 am 17.8.17

A **Operations:-** Our guns fired their usual programme for the day. At 3.30 pm our two guns at M14 c 80-60 and our gun at M14 c 60-80. fired 150 rounds, traversing enemy's support line, which was visible about midway up the row of Dunes about 250 yds behind the barricades approx. M14 b 60.40.

Many direct hits on the trench were obtained. Sandbags, wood and trench material being seen to be thrown into the air.

Enemy retaliation. Nil

B **Enemy defences & organisation**

C **Enemy Activity.**

D **Information**

2 C. Goodall Lt.
for O.C.
"Nieuprock."

Daily Intelligence Summary.

Unit: "Unfrock"

From 6am 17.8.17 to 6am 18.8.17.

A. Operations. At 3pm. we carried out a shoot with 3 guns on enemy Trench systems, visible midway up and along the top of the Pimple about M14 b central. Good results were observed. Direct hits were obtained on a large wooden structure (a dug-out?) visible on the near slope of the pimple wrecking it. 120 Rounds in all were fired.

B. Enemy defences and organisation.

C. Enemy Activity.

D. Information.

S.C. Goodall. Lt.
for OC.

199th L.T.M.B

Daily Intelligence Summary

Unit: Unfrock

From 6 a.m. 18.8.17 to 6 a.m. 19.8.17

A. <u>Operations</u> During the day, Stokes were active at intervals on enemy trench systems in the neighbourhood of the Pimple and M14b. M15a. Accurate shooting was observed.

B. <u>Enemy defences and organisation</u>

C. <u>Enemy Activity</u>

D. <u>Information</u>

                                                          S.C. Goodall. Lt
                                                            for O.C.
                                                        199th L.T.M.B.

Daily Intelligence Summary.

Unit: Unrock.
From 6am 19.8.'17 to 6am 20.8.17.

A/ Operations: Our guns again fired during the day on enemy trench systems in the vicinity of the Temple and M14b. M15a.
Observers report excellent shooting.

B/ Enemy defences & organisation.

C/ Enemy Activity.

D/ Information.

L.C. Goodall Lt.
for O.C.
199th L.T.M.B.

Daily Intelligence Summary

Unit "Munfrock"

From 6am 20.8.17 to 6am 21.8.17.

A. Operations. Our guns fired 125 rounds between 3 & 5 pm on Brushwood covering the Barricade. Accurate observation was impossible owing to heavy shelling of our front line by the Bosch. Observers report many direct hits but difficult to estimate damage done.

B. Enemy defences & organisation.

C. Enemy Activity.

D. Information.

L.C. Goodall Lt
for O.C.
199th L.T.M.B.

Appendix II

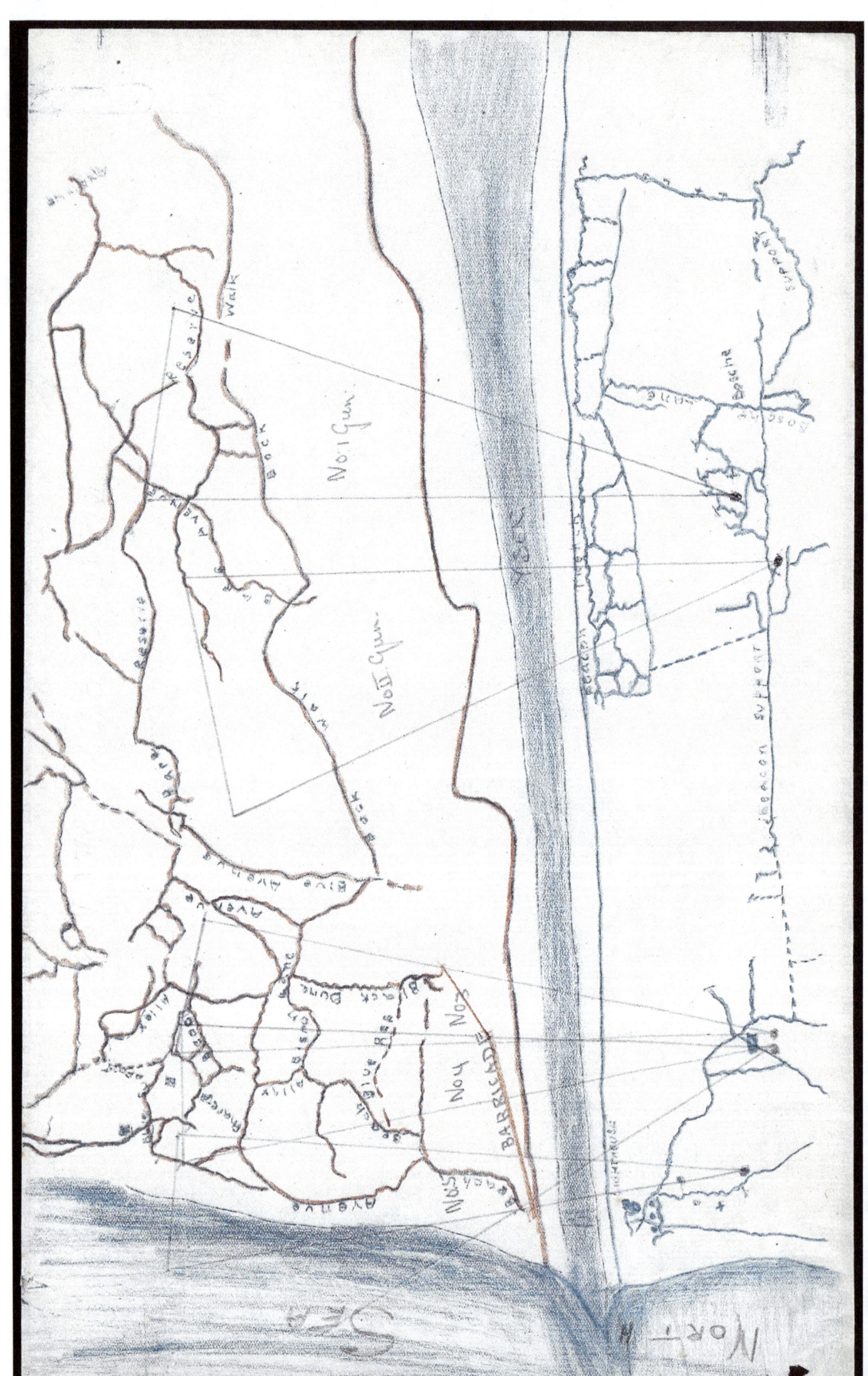

NIEUPORT BAINS SECTOR

Appendix III

Army Form C. 2118

WAR DIARY
or
INTELLIGENCE SUMMARY
(Erase heading not required.)

Instructions regarding War Diaries and Intelligence Summaries are contained in F. S. Regs., Part II. and the Staff Manual respectively. Title Pages will be prepared in manuscript.

Place	Date	Hour	Summary of Events and Information	Remarks and references to Appendices
Coxyde-Bains	1.9.17	10.p.m	Summary of Events for Month of August 1917. During the month of August we were in the line in two sectors, viz:- Nieuport and Nieuport Bains spending 11 days in each. On coming out of the Nieuport sector we rested for a few days in Coxyde Bains and often being relieved in the Nieuport Bains sector we rested in Wulpen camp near Coxyde Bains — Oost Dunkerque Bains road. During the time we were at Nieuport we were unable to fire owing to the extreme artillery activity by both sides by suitable targets and unnecessary danger incurred, owing to there being no trenches or gun-pits — also the ammunition supply was extremely difficult to find up in the line and no clearance even for men was afforded. at the Nieuport Bains sector however many good shoots were done — the firing generally being made on the Palisade, Grey Wall and the Riffle, & this sector useful over 1300 rounds. During the month 9 casualties were received, mostly gas poisoning incurred at Nieuport. The weather became unsettled during the latter part of the month and training were rendered difficult when in rest. Our quarters in Wulpen camp were frequently shelled during the last week. We took part in no offensive action during the month.	

Paul Phillips (?) Capt
O.C. 194th STMB

Army Form C. 2118.

WAR DIARY
or
INTELLIGENCE SUMMARY

(Erase heading not required.)

Place	Date	Hour	Summary of Events and Information	Remarks and references to Appendices
COXYDE BAINS (Wilshire Camp)	Sept 1st		Weather wet. Training. S.E.G. Received Brig. B.O. No.53 Copy No.10	
-"-	2nd		Weather fine. Received Brig: Administrative Order No.53. Copy No.16. S.E.G	
-"-	3rd		Weather fine. Training	S.E.G
-"-	4th		Weather fine. Training. O.C. 197th S.T.M.B visited H.Q. to arrange taking over in accordance with B.O.No53.	S.E.G
CONXYDE BAINS	5th		Weather fine. The Battery moved in accordance with B.O. No53 into billets in CONXYDE BAINS. Move complete by 10 a.m.	S.E.G
-"-	6th		Weather fine. Training	S.E.G
-"-	7th		Weather fine. Training	S.E.G
-"-	8th		Weather fine. Training	S.E.G
-"-	9th		Weather fine. Training	S.E.G

Army Form C. 2118.

WAR DIARY
or
INTELLIGENCE SUMMARY

(Erase heading not required.)

Instructions regarding War Diaries and Intelligence Summaries are contained in F. S. Regs., Part II. and the Staff Manual respectively. Title Pages will be prepared in manuscript.

Place	Date	Hour	Summary of Events and Information	Remarks and references to Appendices
COXYDE BAINS	9/11 10th		Weather fine. Training.	
"	11th		Weather fine. Training.	S.E.G.
"	12th		Weather fine. Training.	S.E.G.
"	13th		Weather fine. Training.	S.E.G.
"	14th		Weather fine. Training.	S.E.G.
"	15th		Weather fine. Training.	S.E.G.
"	16th		Weather fine. Training. O.C. Batt: visited O.C. 198th Battery to arrange relief. Received B.O.O. No. 54 Copy no: 10. Administrative Order no. 19 Bty. no. 16	S.E.G.
"	17th		Weather fine. Training. Received Addendum to B.O.O. no. 54.	S.E.G.
"	18th		Weather wet. No 1 Section relieved section of 198th Battery in the line at NIEUPORT BAINS. Relief complete 11 P.M.	S.E.G.
NIEUPORT BAINS (Middlesex Camp)	19th		Weather unsettled. H.Q. & no 2 Section relieved 198th Batt: in MIDDLESEX CAMP. Relief complete 12.	S.E.G.

Army Form C. 2118.

WAR DIARY
or
INTELLIGENCE SUMMARY
(Erase heading not required.)

Place	Date	Hour	Summary of Events and Information	Remarks and references to Appendices
NIEUPORT BAINS (Sunny Camp)	20th Sept		Weather fine. Our guns fired as stated in T.P.R. S.E.G	T.P.R. 19/9/17 – 20/9/17
" "	21st		Weather fine. Our guns fired as stated in T.P.R. 2/Lt. H.D.M. Campbell taken to C.C.S. (sick). 16 R. taken to C.C.S. (sick) S.E.G	T.P.R. 20/9/17 – 21/9/17
" "	22nd		Weather fine. Our guns fired as stated in T.P.R. S.E.G	
" "	23rd		Weather fine. Our guns were actually taking part in a shoot with the 6" + 2" T.M. as shown in T.P.R. Received B.O.O. no 55 & M.1. 10.10 also A.O. no 20+ S.E.G	T.P.R. 22/9/17 – 23/9/17
" "	24th		Weather fine. Our guns were active as shown in T.P.R. Lut 6 E 19 2 T.M.B. with 2nd taking king round the guns. Handed the Trench down + hut at Sunny Camp in afternoon. he 2 Lieut on muncly stage out + billets in Bayer Bains. T.U. 127 S.T.M.B. handed 101 section with line commencing @ 116 m from field 3 a.m (25/9/17) Relief carried out without casualties although road was being shelled fairly heavily. Received B.O.O. no 56 & M.1. no 56 S.E.G	T.P.R. 23/9/17 – 24/9/17

Army Form C. 2118.

WAR DIARY
or
INTELLIGENCE SUMMARY
(Erase heading not required.)

Instructions regarding War Diaries and Intelligence Summaries are contained in F. S. Regs., Part II. and the Staff Manual respectively. Title Pages will be prepared in manuscript.

Place	Date	Hour	Summary of Events and Information	Remarks and references to Appendices.
CONDE BAINS	Sat 25/11		Weather fine. The Battery marched out in accordance with B.O.O.57. B.O.0.N0 56. Marching through KERKE PANNE - LA PANNE - ADINKERKE - PONT-DE-GHYVELDE to GHYVELDE when we marched @ 9-30 p.m. Regards B.O.57 B.O N0 10	369
GHYVELDE	26th		Weather fine. Received Appendix "B" to B.O.O. 57.	369
—	27th		Weather fine. Billeting party transport proceeded to Rousbrugge Ching in accordance with B.O.O.57	369
—	28th		Weather fine. The Battery embarqued in accordance with B.O.O.57. Commenced @ about 12.45 p.m. Detrained about 6.45 and marched to billets at Heuringhem.	369
HEURING- EN	29th		Weather fine. Training	
—	30th		Weather fine. Training	

Army Form W. 3091.

Cover for Documents.

Nature of Enclosures.

Duplicate   Original

WAR DIARY
of
199th L.T.M.B.
from
1st Oct. – 31st Oct 1917.

VOLUME III

Notes, or Letters written.

APPENDIX

I. T.P.R's.
II. Operation Orders.
III. Casualty Returns
IV. Short Summary of events for month

War Diary

WAR DIARY
or
INTELLIGENCE SUMMARY

(Erase heading not required.)

Army Form C. 2118.

Place	Date	Hour	Summary of Events and Information	Remarks and references to Appendices
HEUREN-GHEN	Oct 1st 1917		Weather fine. Training and seven mile route march in 7 S.M.O. one man sick. Received B.O.O. No. 58 Cdy. No. 10. also Administration Order No. 27 Cdy. No. 10. Covering to B.O.O. No. 58 + BM/419. Attended Conference @ B.H.Q. re Defendline Equipment.	B.O.O. No. 58 Admin Order No. 22 Covering to No. 58 BM/419
"	Oct 2nd		Weather fine. Training in the morning. A.S.C. wagon transports were loaded by 4 p.m. in accordance with S.G/81. The Battery moved out @ 7-45 p.m. marching to cross Rd. Shot of Wallem Capelle where we arrived @ about 12-30 a.m. (3/10/17). Received B.O.O. No. 59 OO own to B.O.O. No. 58. S.G. 77. S.G.80. S.G.81. A @ 31. Q. 60 AS/C. 1+2.	Addendum to B.O.O No. 58 S.G. 77 S.G. 80 S.G. 81 A.Q. 31 Q.S/C 1+2
BRAMD-DEK	" 3rd		Weather just. Bivouaced @ 3-30 a.m. @ Wallem Capelle when we proceeded to get a est in anything then about 4-30 a.m. The Battery intering ken to Brandhoek when it arrived at 2.6 a.m. It then marched to Toronto Camp when it was billeted in huts + under canvas.	

WAR DIARY
or
INTELLIGENCE SUMMARY
(Erase heading not required.)

Army Form C. 2118.

Place	Date	Hour	Summary of Events and Information	Remarks and references to Appendices
BRAND H — OEK (TORONTO CAMP)	Oct 4		Weather wet. Received B.M./422 dated 0.0. 40.59 6 pm 4th Oct. O.C. + 2d i/c attended Brigade Conference.	B.M./422 0.0.40.59
"	5		Weather wet. O.C. Batt. proceeded to the line @ 8 a.m. The Battery marched to Pt Camp @ 10.15 a.m. marching to the Back] Yours where it halted to Zonnen till 3 p.m. We then proceeded to H.9 in the line (POTSDAM) where we met O.C. Batt @ 5.30 p.m. The num. had to go and started relief @ 9.15 p.m. No 1 Section relieved the 11th A.S.T.M.B. in the rt sub sector + No 2 Section the 10th A.S.T.M.B. in left sub sector. Relief complete @ 1 a.m 6/10/17. Our guns cooperated with the Artillery in answer to S.O.S. signals which were sent up twice during the night. Much difficulty was experienced in the relief owing to the Darkness nature of the ground. Relief complete without a casualty.	269 264

Army Form C. 2118.

WAR DIARY
or
INTELLIGENCE SUMMARY
(Erase heading not required.)

Place	Date	Hour	Summary of Events and Information	Remarks and references to Appendices
YPRES	Oct 6 1917		Weather v. wet. Gun teams dug themselves in, making cover from if time both for themselves & guns. Day quiet.	S.6.y
ZONNEBEKE	Oct 7		Weather v. wet. O.C. 7th A.S.T.M.B. visited our H.Q. (POTSDAM) in the early morning taking our guns on the right sub-section. Received B.O.O. no 60 & by 7 relief in accordance with B.O.O. no: 60 complete @ 6.30 A.M. No Section came to H.Q. Our guns fired in reply to S.O.S. Gas fired 50 rounds amongst a large party of the enemy who were assembling in the Cemetery. Many more seen to fall. The remainder to disperse.	S.6.y B.O.O no: 60
	8/7		Weather very wet. Oct 4.30 p.m. No 3 Section were withdrawn from the front line and the whole of at Battery assembled on Hill 40 to take up pack part position. Battery complete on Hill 40 by 9.30 p.m. 10.? casualty. Communication was & now organise with the 57th Manchester Regt.	S.6.y

Army Form C. 2118.

WAR DIARY
or
INTELLIGENCE SUMMARY

(Erase heading not required.)

Instructions regarding War Diaries and Intelligence Summaries are contained in F.S. Regs., Part II. and the Staff Manual respectively. Title Pages will be prepared in manuscript.

Place	Date	Hour	Summary of Events and Information	Remarks and references to Appendices
ZONNEBEKE	Oct 9th 1919		Weather wet. Battery remained in support on HILL 40. All ours were received @ 4pm to return to POTSDAM when Battery was complete by 9 p.m. Casualties – O.R. 3 ky.	
ANDHOEK (TORONTO CAMP)	Oct 10th		Weather wet. The Battery marched out from H.9. (POTSDAM) (PETROGRAD) by Sections commanded @ 4 P.M. Battery Sections left 3 mm – 1/4 6.0 follows with O.C Battery to wait for transport for guns. All Battery movies near path complete @ TORONTO CAMP by 9 p.m.	3 ky
	11th	1-30 P.M.	Weather wet. Remainder of the Battery with transport marched to TORONTO CAMP by 1-30 P.M.	3 ky
	12th		Weather wet. Received Brigade warning Order No B.M/503. Also S.C 35. B.0.0 No. 61 & by No. 10.	B.M/503 S.C/35 B.0.0 No 61

Army Form C. 2118.

WAR DIARY
or
INTELLIGENCE SUMMARY
(Erase heading not required.)

Instructions regarding War Diaries and Intelligence Summaries are contained in F. S. Regs., Part II. and the Staff Manual respectively. Title Pages will be prepared in manuscript.

Place	Date	Hour	Summary of Events and Information	Remarks and references to Appendices
BRANDHOEK (TORONTO CAMP)	Oct 13th		Weather wet. Made in aeroplanes with B.O.O. W. 61. The Battery marched to VLAMERTINGE STATION where we were to entrain at 8 a.m. We loaded the 1st Line Transport and individually entrained at 3 p.m. Reached ARQUES at about 9-30 p.m. & off loaded the transport and marched to billets at MALHOVE where we reached @ 1-30 a.m. (14/10/17) S.G.	
MALHOVE, ARQUES	14th		Weather fine. S.G.	
	15th		Weather fine. Training. S.G.	
	16th		Weather fine. Training. S.G.	
	17th		Weather fine. Training. S.G.	
	18th		Weather fine. Training. S.G.	

WAR DIARY
or
INTELLIGENCE SUMMARY

Army Form C. 2118.

Place	Date	Hour	Summary of Events and Information	Remarks and references to Appendices
RUE MALHOVE ARQUES.	Oct 19th		Weather fine. Training. Received A.2318 (Brig.of.the.Batt.n)	A.2318
CAMPAGNE	"20"		Weather fine. marched out of MALHOVE @ 2.15 p.m. in accordance with A.2318. Arrived ARQUES to CAMPAGNE where we marched by 3-30 p.m. &c.9. On arrival ordered military road. (S.No 61394)	&c.9
	"21st"		Weather fine. Church Parade.	&c.9
	"22nd"		Weather fine. Training.	&c.9
	"23rd"		Weather wet. Training.	&c.9
	"24th"		Weather fine. Training. Received movement order No A.2405.	A.2405 &c.9
	"25th"		Weather wet. The Battn. made in accordance with movement order A.2405 to Rue MALHOVE, ARQUES, arriving there @ 4-30 p.m.	&c.9

WAR DIARY
or
INTELLIGENCE SUMMARY

(Erase heading not required.)

Army Form C. 2118.

Place	Date	Hour	Summary of Events and Information	Remarks and references to Appendices
RUE MALHOVE ARQUES	Oct		Weather wet. Training	
	27th		Weather fine. Training	S.G.G.
	28th		Weather fine. Church parade in morning. Received D.D.M.63 GS No 1010.	S.G.G.
	29th		Weather fine. The Battery marched out in billets at 9 AM and took up position on the ARQUES-AIRE road where they were inspected by the Commander-in-Chief and afterwards marched past him.	A.O.Oka-62 S.G.G.
	30th		Weather wet. The Battery took part in a Brigade Scheme which was ordered by the men. Received D.O.O. No-63 G.S.HY/b	R.O. No-63
	31st		Weather fine. The Battery formed up in the square ARQUES in marching order D.D.M.63 when the O.C presented medal ribbons. Received Downing Order. B.M. 558/2.	B.S 341

Tactical Progress Reports.

Daily Intelligence Summary

Unit "Unfrock"

Information

1. About 7 p.m. in response to S.O.S. from our infantry, our gun at D.16.b.45.68 fired 50 rounds on the western edge of Augustus Wood and our gun at D.16.b.50.68 fired 10 rounds on the cemetery at D.17.a.60.20.

Nothing further to report.

Enemy Activity

Enemy Defences & Organisation

S.G. Goodall Lieut.
for O.C
199th L.T.M.B

Daily Intelligence Summary.

Unit: Mufrock

Information

Stokes fired in co-operation with the artillery during the day.

The night passed fairly quietly.

Enemy Activity

Enemy Defences & Organisation.

J C Goodall Lieut
for O.C.
Mufrock.

Operation Orders

Copy No. 10

199th Infantry Brigade.
Administration Order No. ....22.

1/10/17.

Ref; 199th Brigade Operation Order No. 57.
" Maps.- HAZEBROUCK "A"
    Sheets 27)
         56a) 1/40.000

BAGGAGE. 1. Baggage Wagons will be sent to Units 18 hours before move, Horses and Drivers returning to Company Lines.

RATIONS. 2. (i) Rations for consumption for day of moves will be carried by Units.

(ii) Rations for consumption following day will be loaded on Supply Wagon, from present Dump, on the evening prior to respective moves. Loaded Wagons will return to, and Park in, Company Lines. Wagons will move with Company and will deliver Rations to Units upon arrival in KECKE Area.

TRANSPORT. 3. The following additional Transport has been allotted to Units for carrying Blankets, Surplus Kit, Etc.

```
2/5th Manchesters.........1½ Lorries.
2/6th Manchesters.........1½    "
2/7th Manchesters.........1½    "
2/8th Manchesters.........1½    "
199th Brigade H.Q.........1     "
2/3rd Field Ambulance.....1     "
199th L.T.M.Battery.......1 G.S.Wagon.
```

4. ACKNOWLEDGE.

Gerald Unsworth Captain.
Staff Captain.
199th Infantry Brigade.

DISTRIBUTION.

```
Copy No. 1.....Brigadier-General.
         2.....Brigade Major.
         3.....Staff Captain.
         4.....199th Brigade Signals.
         5.....O.C. 2/5th Manchesters.
         6.....  "   2/6th    "
         7.....  "   2/7th    "
         8.....  "   2/8th    "
         9.....  "   204th M.G.Company.
        10.....  "   199th L.T.M.Battery.
        11.....
        12.....  "   2/3rd Field Ambulance.
        13.....  "   544 Company A.S.C.
        14.....66th Division "Q"
        15.....199th Brigade Q.M.S.
        16.....Q.M.2/5th Manchesters.
        17.....  "   2/6th    "
        18.....  "   2/7th    "
        19.....  "   2/8th    "
```

20........432nd Field Company.
21........66th Divisional Train.
22........S.S.O., 66th Division.
23........S.O., 199th Brigade.
24........File.
25........War Diary.
26........)
27........)
28........) SPARE.

SECRET
199 LTMB

199TH INFANTRY BDE
No. BM/419
Date............

Ref. 199 Inf Bde order no 58,
the move on Oct 3rd may be postponed.
Advance parties will therefore parade
at WARDRECQUES at 2.0 pm tomorrow
instead of 8.0 am, in case orders for
postponement are received.

R.H. Bond
Capt.
B/Major 199 Inf.? Bde

1.10.17

No. 10.

CORRECTION
to
199th BRIGADE ORDER No. 58.

MARCH TABLE.   Brigade Starting point Column 2 and Column 4 should read B.8.a.75.60 not A.8.a.75.60.

R.W.Bond
Captain.
Brigade Major.
199th Infantry Brigade.

BHQ.
1-10-17.

Distribution:-
To all recipients of OO.58.

ADDENDUM to 199th INFANTRY BRIGADE

OPERATION ORDER NO:58.
---

1. The 199th Infantry Brigade will move as arranged tomorrow to the EECKE area where it will entrain.

2. Billeting parties are to stand by pending further orders.

Gerald Unsworth Captain.
for Brigade Major.
199th Infantry Brigade.

B.H.Q.
3.10.17.

DISTRIBUTION:-

    To all recipients of OO.58 of 1.10.17.

199th Infantry Brigade   Copy No. 10

ADDENDUM to Operation Order No. 58

2.10.17.

Ref MAPS   HAZEBROUCK 'A'.

Sheets 27)
       36a) 1/40.000

TRANSPORT. 1. The Transport of the 199th Infantry Brigade will move as a Brigade Group from WARDRECQUES to EECKE Area to-day the 2nd instant, under the Command of Captain SANDILANDS O.C. 544 Company A.S.C.

ROUTE. 2. The route will be as detailed in March Table accompanying Operation Order No. 58 of 1.10.17.

STARTING POINT. 3. The Starting Point will be the Square opposite Church WARDRECQUES (A.6.d.8.4.)

STARTING TIMES. 4. Units will pass this point at the following times :-

- 544 Company A.S.C.............4.30 p.m.
- 199th Brigade H.Qrs..........4.35 p.m.
- 2/5th Manchesters............4.40 p.m.
- 2/7th Manchesters............4.45 p.m.
- 2/8th Manchesters............4.50 p.m.
- 2/6th Manchesters............4.55 p.m.
- 204 M.G.Company..............5.0 p.m.
- 2/3rd Field Ambulance........5.5.p.m.

RATIONS. 5. The unexpended portion of to-days Rations and Rations for the 3rd instant will be carried.

POSITIONS. 6. Officers Commanding will take steps to ensure that their Transport debauches on to the road in its correct position as regards other Units.

MARCH DISCIPLINE. 7. Particular attention is to be paid to march discipline.

TRANSPORT - LOADING OF. 8. The attention of Units is drawn to the fact that Transport must NOT be over-loaded. The march being a long one it is necessary to conserve as far as possible the energies of the Transport animals. The Brigadier-General wishes Commanding Officers to give this matter their personal attention.

INTERVALS. 9. The following intervals will be kept :- 100 yards between each Unit Transport and 500 yards between 2/8th Battn; and 2/6th Battalion.

BILLETING PARTIES. 10. 2 men per Unit on cycles as advanced billeting party will report to an N.C.O. of 544 Company A.S.C. at Brigade Headquarters at 2.30 p.m to-day.
On arrival the advanced party will report to the Staff Captain's representative at the road junction near the Church at ST. SYLVESTRE CAPPEL (P.23.c.7.0).

GUIDES. 11. Guides from advanced parties will meet Transport at cross roads (P.35.b.5.2) at 11-0 p.m.

(continued)

12. The Brigade Transport Group will proceed on the morning of the 3rd instant to the BRANDHOEK Area.

13. ACKNOWLEDGE.

R.I.Rand
~~Brigade Staff~~ Captain.

DISTRIBUTION.

No.....1 Brigadier-General.
2. Brigade Major.
3. Staff Captain.
4. 66th Division "Q"
5. 2/5th Manchesters
6. 2/6th Manchesters
7. 2/7th Manchesters.
8. 2/8th Manchesters
9. 204th M.G. Company.
10. 199th L.T.M. Battery.
11. 66th Division "G"
12. "   "   "A"
13. ...)
14. ...) O.C. 544 Company A.S.C.
15. 2/3rd Field Ambulance
16. O.M. 2/5th Manchesters.
17. "   2/6th Manchesters.
18. "   2/7th Manchesters.
19. "   2/8th Manchesters.
20. 199th Brigade Q.M.S.
21. 432nd Field Company.
22. S.S.O. 66th Division.
23. S.O. 199th Brigade.
24. File.
25. ...)
26. ...) War Diary.
27. ......)
28. ......) Spare.

SECRET.   Copy No. 10.

199th Infantry Brigade
ORDER No: 58.

Ref: Maps.   HAZEBROUCK 5A.

   Sheet 27)
     "   36A) 1/40,000.

1. The 66th Division (less Artillery, R.E. and Pioneer Battalion) will move from the RENESCURE area to the EECKE area on the 1st, 2nd and 3rd of October.

2. The 199th Infantry Brigade Group will move to the EECKE area (Western sub area) on October 3rd.

3. A march table is attached.

4. Distances as laid down in 199th Infantry Brigade G.466, 29-9-17, are to be observed on the march. There will be a distance of 100 yards in rear of L.T.M.B., and 100 yards in rear of M.G.Coy. and 500 yards in rear of 2/3rd Field Ambulance.

5. 1st Line Transport and 2nd line Baggage wagons will march with units. Supply wagons will march with the train company.

6. Advance parties from all units will proceed to the new area on October 2nd. at least two members of each Battalion party will be mounted on bicycles. The whole of the advance parties will rendezvous at the main square WARDRECQUES at 8.0 a.m. on the 2nd October whence dismounted personnel will be marched under an officer (to be detailed by O.C, 2/5th Manch.Regt) to ST.SYLVESTRE CAPPEL. This party will meet the Staff Captain at the road junction near the church P.23.c.7.0 on arrival.

7. Guides from advance parties will meet units at cross roads P.35.b.5.2. at 2.0 p.m. on 3.10.17.

8. Brigade Headquarters will close at WARDRECQUES at 7.45 a.m. on October 3rd. and reopen at ST.SYLVESTRE CAPPEL on arrival.

9. Units **must** send in map location of H.Q. immediately on arrival.

10. The Division will move to the WINNEZEELE area on October 4th. The 199th Infantry Brigade will move in the afternoon.

11. ACKNOWLEDGE.

                                                R W Bond
                                                   Captain,
B.H.Q.   Brigade Major,
1.10.17.   199th Infantry Brigade.

Distribution :-

Copy No. 1...Brig-General.   Copy No. 11..2/3rd Field Amb.
  "   "   2...Brigade Major.   "   "   12..544 Coy. A.S.C.
  "   "   3...Staff Captain.   "   "   13..66th Division, "G"
  "   "   4...Brigade Sig. Officer.   "   "   14..   "   "A"
  "   "   5...O.C, 2/5th Manch.Regt.   "   "   15..War Diary.
  "   "   6...O.C, 2/6th   "   "   "   "   16..
  "   "   7...O.C, 2/7th   "   "   "   "   17..File.
  "   "   8...O.C, 2/8th   "   "   "   "   18..Spare.
  "   "   9...O.C, 204th M.G.Coy.   "   "   19..   "
  "   " 10...199th L.T.M. Battery.

MARCH TABLE to accompany 199th Infantry Brigade

ORDER No: 58.

Units in order of march.	Starting point.	Time.	Time at Brigade S.P.	Route.	Remarks:
Brigade H.Q.	Rd.junction B.8.a.75.60.	6.0 a.m.	6.0 a.m.	PONT ASQUIN - X roads B.2.b.9.0 - LYNDE - WALLON CAPPEL - Road junction U.24.c.2.8. - Level crossing at LA HTE LOGE - X roads V.21.d.5.2. - X roads V.32.b.0.2. - ST.SYLVESTRE CAPPEL.	
2/5th Manch.Regt.	"	6.3 a.m.	6.3 a.m.		
2/7th "	A.24.a.70.90.	7.41 a.m.	8.20 a.m.		
2/8th "	"	8.08 a.m.	8.37 a.m.		
2/6th "	A.9.d.7.1.	8.30 a.m.	9.4 a.m.		
199th L.T.M.B.	"	8.17 a.m.	9.21 a.m.		199th L.T.M.B. will arrange to leave HEURINGHEM in rear of 2/6th Manch.Regt.
204th M.G.Coy.	A.8.a.75.60.	9.24 a.m.	9.24 a.m.		
2/3rd Fld. Amb.	"	9.31 a.m.	9.31 a.m.		Motor ambulances will move independently under orders of O.C. 2/3rd Fld.Ambulance.
544 Coy. A.S.C.	"	9.42 a.m.	9.42 a.m.		

"A" Form.
MESSAGES AND SIGNALS.

Army Form C. 2121.
(In pads of 100.)

Sender's Number.	Day of Month.	In reply to Number.	AAA
AS/C.1	2		

2/6th Manchesters will embus at the M of Compagne on the main ARQUES-AIRE Road at 6.30pm today AAA Following parties of men unable to march in accordance with return rendered to day will report to O.C. 2/6th Manchesters at embussing point at 6.30pm AAA 2/5th Manchesters 41 O.R, 2/7th Manchesters 64 O.R. 2/8th 33 O.R. AAA They will proceed to Saint Sylvestre Cappel to billet for the night Billeting parties on arrival of Battn will report to Lieut Ellis A/S.C at the

"A" Form.
MESSAGES AND SIGNALS.

Army Form C. 2121.
(In pads of 100.)

Sender's Number.	Day of Month.	In reply to Number.	AAA
AS/C1	2		

Church at Saint Sylvestre Cappel AAA Blankets to accompany men on busses AAA Lorry will be at HEURENGHEN to-morrow morning to bring surplus stores of 2/6th Manchesters and 6.T.M.B. AAA. O.C. 2/6th Manchesters will arrange to have his Battalion and attached units at CAESTRE railway Stn at 8 a.m. One officer and rear party will be left behind to come with lorry AAA

"A" Form.
MESSAGES AND SIGNALS.

Army Form C. 2121.
(In pads of 100.)

Sender's Number.	Day of Month.	In reply to Number.	AAA
AS/C2	2		

2/7th Manchesters and L.T.M.B. are to be on the main HAZEBRUCK ROAD at EBLINGHEM Sh Square E.4. Ref Map Sh HAZEBRUCK by 10:30pm to night ready to embus AAA They will travel by 7am train from CAESTRE tomorrow bivouacing at Station 3 lorries will be available tomorrow morning time unknown to carry blankets and surplus stores of 2/7th and 2/8 Manchesters AAA Party of 1 Officer and 6 O.R. to be left by each unit and brought by the lorry AAA L.T.M.B. will move in rear of 2/7th MR

"A" Form.
MESSAGES AND SIGNALS.

Army Form C. 2121
(in pads of 100).

TO { UNFROCK

Sender's Number.	Day of Month.	In reply to Number.	A A A
AD31	2		

In continuation our JC 80 personnel of Units will be ready to move at 7 pm this evening and Orders for Transport already issued

From Anfair

Army Form C. 2121.
(In pads of 100.)

TO	UNFOLD	UNFURL	UNFIT	UNFROCK

Sender's Number.	Day of Month.	In reply to Number.	AAA
S.C. 81.	2.		

Men	are	to	leave
tea	not	later	than
4 p.m.	today	...	dixies
are	to	be	carried
on	the	lorries	allotted
to	units	and	not
taken	with	transport	...
The	lorry	allotted	to
UNFOLD	will	carry	dixies
for	UNFROCK	...	Lorry
allotted	to	Brigade	H.Q.
will	carry	dixies	for
204 Machine	Guns	and	2/5 Field
Ambulance	...	Addressed	UNFOLD
UNFURL	UNFIT	UNFROCK	

From
Place
Time

The above may be forwarded as now corrected. (Z)

MESSAGES AND SIGNALS.

Form C. 2121.

TO: UNFIX UNFELT UNFROCK

Sender's Number: S.C. 80
Day of Month: 2.

Instructions have been received that the Brigade must proceed to prepared to EECKE Area by bus on march route this afternoon the 2nd inst and to be in readiness from 4 pm onwards

From: UNFAIR

"A" Form.
MESSAGES AND SIGNALS.

Army Form C. 2121.
(In pads of 100.)

Prefix	Code	m	Words	Charge	This message is on a/c of:	Recd. at .... m.
Office of Origin and Service Instructions. SDR		Sent At .....m. To...... By......			........................Service. (Signature of "Franking Officer.")	Date........ From........ By........

TO ~~Unfair~~ ~~Unfold~~ Unfrock

Sender's Number. SC 77	Day of Month. 2	In reply to Number.	A A A
spent	will	move	to
ERCKE	Area	40 h.m.	today
~~this~~	Unexpected	portion	of
todays	rations	and	rations
for	tomorrow	3rd inst	to
~~be~~	taken	~~this~~	detailed
Orders	will	follow	~~this~~

From: Unfair
Place:
Time: 1140

The above may be forwarded as now corrected. (Z)

SECRET.   199. INF. BDE.   ORDER. No 59.   Copy No. 6
Ref. 1/40000 sheet 28.

1. The BDE. FRONT. will be from D23 d 8.8
   to D10 d 3.0
2. 2/5 MANCH. REGT. & 2/8th MANCH. REGT.
   will relieve the Right & Left BDES. 3rd
   Australian DIV. in front line on the night
   5/6th Oct.
3. 2/6th MANCH. REGT. & 2/7th MANCH. REGT.
   will be in support. 2/6th Manch Regt
   on the Right.
4. 2/6 MANCH Regt. 2/7th MANCH REGT.
   204 MG Coy & L.TMB will move in
   the above order from BRANDHOEK on
   Oct 5th.
   Starting Point. BDE HQ H7 d 1.1
   Heads to pass starting point:-
      2/6 MANCH. Regt.   9.0 am
      2/7 "   9.18 "
      204 M.G.C.   9.36 "
      L.TMB.   9.40 "
5. 1st line transport will accompany Units
6. The Column will halt with head at
   H12 d 6.5 until arrival of COs.
   after completion of preliminary
   reconnaissance & will then move to
   Bivouac East of YPRES
7. Orders for relief will be issued later.

4.9.17.   P.T.O.   M. ?
   Capt. Bde Maj
   199 Inf Bde

Distribution.

1. BDE.
2. 1/- MANCH. REGT.
3. 2/6 " "
4. 2/7 " "
5. 2/8 " "
6. 204 M.G.C.
7. 199. LTMB.
8. 3rd Reserve Div.

BM/422

O.C. 2/6th Manch. Regt.
" 2/7th "
204 M.G. Coy
199 L.T.M.B.

1. The 199th Inf Bde will relieve two Bde of 3rd Australian Div. tomorrow night 5/6th Oct. in front line.

2. The above four Units will hold themselves in readiness to proceed at one hours notice to the East of YPRES. It is hoped to provide tram or bus as far as YPRES.

3. 3 representatives from Each battalion
   1 " " M.G. Coy.
   1 " " L.T.M.B.
   can be conveyed to new Bde H.Q. Besseins Stores from 3rd Div. Xpram hamm Dump near the Prisoners of War Cage by Motor Lorry.
   To report at the Dump at 8.15 am.

4. COs. 2nd in Command & Adjt. to report at Bde H.Q. at 6.30 am. COs will proceed to the line with Bde Maj. by Car.

5. Detailed orders will be issued as soon as possible.

4-10-17.

M Boyd
Capt Bde Maj.
199 Inf Bde.

"A" Form.
MESSAGES AND SIGNALS.

Army Form C. 2121
(in pads of 100).

TO	2/5 Manchester 2/3 Manchester	2/3 Field
	2/6 " L.T.M.B.	Amb
	2/7 " 204 M.G. Coy	544 Coy A.S.C

Sender's Number.	Day of Month.	In reply to Number.	AAA
S.C. 35	12th		

Urgently required entraining strength of your unit. aaa You must be prepared to entrain at 7.45 a.m at BRANDHOEK aaa Four wheeled transport proceeds by road aaa Remaining transport including limbers entrains VLAMERTINGHE at 8 a.m.

From: 199 Inf Bde
Place:
Time: 6.30 p.m

Signature: Gnas Unsworth Capt
Staff Capt

O.C.
199th L.T.M.B.

The Baggage wagons reporting to you to-night will be called for at 7 a.m. to-morrow, the 13th inst.

It is essential that these wagons should be ready to draw out at that hour please

_____ Capt.
a/c No. 544 Company ASC

In the Field
12/10/17

199 2 TMB   4M/583

WARNING ORDER

1. The 199 Inf Bde will move tomorrow to Ervillers area.

2. Batteries, Section A & B section + 2 pn attn wagons will stand by ready to move at 2 minutes notice.

3. The Brigade will probably move by Brigade.

                                    R Morris
                                    Capt
                                    Comdg 199 L.T.M.B

12.10.17

SECRET.   Copy No. 7

199 Bde Order No. 60

1. The following readjustment of the front line will take place tonight. Right Bde front 199 Inf. Bde will become left Batt. front 7th A.I Bde.

2. The 2/5th M/c Regt will be relieved by the 25th A Bde, & the 2/6th M/c Regt " " " " 26th A. Bde.

3. Details of relief will be arranged between O/Cs concerned.

4. (a) On relief 2/5th M/c Regt (less 1 Coy) will move on the left of the Railway Line, & Batt will be in support of 2/7th M/c Regt (Coy now on left of line Standing fast)
(b) The 2/6th M/c Regt will relieve the right support Batt of the 147 Bde (49 Div) in the support line, & will be in support of the 28th Infy Regt who are relieving the front line Batt of the same brigade.

5. The 204 MG Coy positions & 199 LTMB positions E of Railway line will be taken over by the 7d AMGC & 7th ALTMB respectively. Details to be arranged between O/Cs concerned.

6. Relief to be complete by 5 AM 7th inst.

7. Acknowledge.

C H Fox Capt.
For Brigade Major
199 Inf. Bde.

Copy No 1. Bde H.Q.
    2. 2/5 Infy Regt
    3. 2/6 "
    4. 7th A.I Bde
    5. 61 Div G
    6. 204 MG Coy
    7. 199 LTMB

SECRET.   Copy No. 10

199th Infantry Brigade
ORDER No: 61.

Ref: HAZEBROUCK 5A.

    Sheet 27)
) 1/40,000.
    Sheet 28)

1. (a) The 199th Infantry Brigade Group will move to the RENESCURE area on 13th October.

   (b) Personnel and a portion of transport will move by train from BRANDHOEK at 7.45 a.m. Remainder of transport will move by march route.

2. The Brigade will entrain at G.5.d.00 (the same place as that at which it detrained before) at 7.45 a.m.

3. Adjutants with markers and entraining states will meet the Brigade Major at G.5.d.00 at 7.30 a.m.

4. Units will arrive at G.5.d.00 in the following order and at the following times :-

         2/5th Manch. Regt.   7.45 a.m.
         2/8th   "   "   7.55 a.m.
         2/7th   "   "   8.05 a.m.
         2/6th   "   "   8.15 a.m.
         204th M.G. Coy.   8.25 a.m.
         2/3rd Field Amb.   8.30 a.m.

5. To allow ample transport for units, blankets will be carried on the man to point of entrainment. At ARQUES blankets will be rolled in bundles of 10, and left at the station under a guard to be detailed by each unit, and will be carried from there by transport under arrangements to be made by Staff Captain.

6. Location returns must be sent in immediately on arrival.

7. (a) The following 1st Line Transport will be ready to entrain at VLAMERTINGHE STATION at 8.0 a.m.

		Horses.
Brigade Headquarters.	1 cooks limber,	2.
Each Battalion.	4 cookers.	32.
	2 water carts.	16.
	1 S.A.A. limber.	8.
	1 mess cart.	4.
Signal Section.	1 Maltese cart.	2.
	1 limbered G.S. wagon.	2.
Machine Gun Coy.	1 water cart.	2.
	1 cooks cart.	2.
	1 H.C. limber.	2.
		72.
L.T.M. Battery.	All hand carts.	

(b) Accommodation available.

    17 flats   = 68 axles.
    21 covered
        wagons. = 161 horses.

(-2-).

7 continued.

Units may send riding and spare horses up to the following numbers by train:-

Brigade Headquarters.	7 Horses.
Each Battalion.	13 "
Signal Section.	4 "
Machine Gun Coy.	11 "
Field Amb.	12 "

 (c) L.T.M.B. personnel will proceed by this train and will be responsible for loading all transport.

 (d) Brigade Transport Officer will be in charge of Transport in Transport Train and superintend loading and unloading.

8. Remainder of transport proceeds by road to RENESCURE area. It will billet on the night of 13/14th in the ~~EECKE~~ area. Report for billets to Area Commandant, ~~EECKE~~. STEENVOORDE. PANSGAT (G.1.C.)

 Route POPERINGHE - ABEELE - ~~GODSWAERSVELDE~~. STEENVOORDE

 Starting point Cross Roads G.17.c.6.9.

 Order of march and time of passing starting point

2/8th Manch.Regt.	10.0 a.m.
2/5th " "	10.5 a.m.
2/7th " "	10.10 a.m.
2/6th " "	10.15 a.m.
Machine Gun Coy.	10.20 a.m.
Brigade H.Q.	10.22 a.m.
Field Ambulance.	10.24 a.m.
544 Coy. A.S.C.	10.29 a.m.

N.B. Baggage waggons will be called for at 7.0 a.m. on 13th. It is essential that they should be ready at this time.

 O.C. 544 Coy. A.S.C. will command the column.

9. The unexpended portion of the day's rations will be carried on the man.
Rations for the 14th. will be dumped in the new area by A.S.C. and drawn by units with limbers and mess carts on arrival.
Rations for the 15th. will be drawn by the train company on the afternoon of the 14th. from railhead at EBBLINGHEM and delivered to units.
The portion of transport proceeding by march route will carry rations for the 14th. with it, in addition to unexpended portion of the day's ration.

10. <u>Motor lorries.</u> 1 lorry will be allotted to each Battalion (except 2/6th Manch.Regt. who will have 2 lorries) and 1 for L.T.M.B. and Machine Gun Coy. together, and 1 for Brigade Laundry.
Time of arrival of lorries will be notified later.

11. Each unit must detail a billeting party of 1 officer and 6 men to proceed by lorry.
544 Coy. A.S.C. billeting party will report at B.H.Q. (H.7.a.11) at 8.0 a.m. to proceed by lorry.

12. All duties and working parties found by 2/6th Manch.Regt. will be taken over by 198th Infantry Brigade tomorrow.
Details relieved will probably proceed to BRANDHOEK on the 13th. continue to RENESCURE area on the 14th. Orders for this move will be issued later by 66th Division, (A).

13. ACKNOWLEDGE.

B.H.Q.
12.10.17.

R L Bond
Captain,
Brigade Major,
199th Infantry Brigade.

Distribution :-

Copy No. 1....Brigadier-General.
 "   " 2....Brigade Major.
 "   " 3....Staff Captain.
 "   " 4....Brigade Sig. Officer.
 "   " 5....O.C, 2/5th Manch.Regt.
 "   " 6....   2/6th   "   "
 "   " 7....   2/7th   "   "
 "   " 8....   2/8th   "   "
 "   " 9....   204th M.G.Coy.
 "   " 10...   199th L.T.M.Battery.
 "   " 11...   2/3rd Field Amb.
 "   " 12...   544 Coy. A.S.C.
 "   " 13...66th Division, "G"
 "   " 14...   "   "   "A"
 "   " 15...198th Infantry Brigade.
 "   " 16...O.C. Divisional Train.
 "   " 17...War Diary.
 "   " 18... "   "
 "   " 19...File.
 "   " 20...Spare.
 "   " 21... "

O.C, 2/5th Bn Manchester Regt.
     2/6th "   "   "
     2/7th "   "   "
     2/8th "   "   "
     204th Machine Gun Coy.
     199th L.T.M. Battery.
HQ., 66th Division.
O.C, 544 Coy. A.S.C.

1.   The 204th Machine Gun Coy. and 199th L.T.M. Battery will move on the 20th inst. to billets in COMPAGNE (S.30.c. ref. Sheet 27) allotted to them by the Area Commandant, RENESCURE, and be clear of ARQUES by 3 p.m.

2. (a) The billets at ARQUES vacated by the 199th L.T.M. Battery will be taken over by the 2/8th Manchester Regt.
   (b) The billets vacated by the 204th Machine Gun Coy. will be taken over by the 2/5th Manchester Regt. and 2/7th Manchester Regt. Representatives of these two battalions will meet the A/Staff Captain at the Headquarters of the 204th Machine Gun Coy. at 10.30 a.m.

3.   ACKNOWLEDGE.

                                    Captain,
                               Staff Captain,
                        199th Infantry Brigade.

B.H.Q.
19.10.17.

MOVE.

199th Infantry Brigade.
MOVEMENT ORDER.

1. The 204th Machine Gun Coy. and L.T.M.B. 199th Infantry Brigade, will move from CAMPAGNE tomorrow the 25th October to take over billets in Rue MALHOVE, ARQUES.

   They will be clear of CAMPAGNE by 3 p.m.

   Billeting parties will report to A/Staff Captain, at Brigade Headquarters at 10 a.m.

TRANSPORT. 2. 2/5th, 2/6th, 2/7th and 2/8th Bns. Manchester Regt. will each detail 2 limbers to report to H.Q. L.T.M.B. at S.30.b.8.8 (Sheet 27) at 2 p.m. tomorrow the 25th instant, to provide transport for guns, ammunition and stores.

3. ACKNOWLEDGE.

\[signature\]
Captain,
Staff Captain,
199th Infantry Brigade.

B.H.Q.
24.10.17.

66th Division. (For information).
544 Coy A.S.C.   "   "
2/5th Manch.Regt.
2/6th   "   "
2/7th   "   "
2/8th   "   "
199th L.T.M.B.
204th M.G.Coy.

Copy No. 10

199th Infantry Brigade
ORDER No. 82.

Ref: Maps. Sheet 27)
              " 36A) 1/40.000.

INSPECTION. 1. The Commander-in-Chief will inspect the Division (less R.A. and A.S.C.) on Monday Oct. 29th. commencing at 11.0 a.m.

DETAILS OF INSPECTION. 2. (a) The 199th Infantry Brigade Group will be drawn up in line on north side of the main ARQUES - AIRE road, ready for inspection at 11.10 a.m. A diagram showing order and road spaces is attached. The Commander-in-Chief in inspecting the Brigade will move from the left flank to the right of the Brigade.

(b) The 199th Infantry Brigade Group will occupy the ground vacated by the 197th Infantry Brigade group immediately the latter has moved off to march past the Commander-in-Chief. The 199th Infantry Brigade group will be formed up in the BATAVIA CHAU. grounds ready to move into position by 10.45 a.m. Adjutants and markers will meet the Brigade Major at the entrance to the chateau grounds, S.22.c.2.8. (just opposite 2/6th Manch.Regt.H.Q.) at 9.45 a.m.

(c) A table is attached showing times of arrival of units at S.22.c.2.8.   10-15 AM

(d) No vehicles will parade.

(e) Dress - "Fighting Order" (with haversacks on the back and shrapnel helmets). Box Respirators will not be carried. Parade will be as strong as possible.

(f) Ranks will be closed. Bayonets fixed.

(g) Two paces between companies, ten paces between battalions, and five paces between other units of Brigade Group.

(h) Road junctions will be left clear.

(i) Brigadiers and Staff, C.Os. and seconds-in-command and adjutants only will be mounted.

(k) Infantry Brigadiers, Battalion Commanders and Os.C. other units of Brigade Group will parade on the left flank of their commands. Commanding Officers will give the general salute and accompany the Commander-in-Chief during his inspection of their own units.

(l) All other officers not referred to in 'k' will stand two paces in front of the centre of their commands.

(m) Platoons are on no account to be split up.

DETAILS OF MARCH PAST. 3. (a) Immediately after the inspection units will march past in column of route with bayonets fixed.

(b) Distances as laid down in I.T. Sec.98 para C will be maintained.

(-2-).

DETAILS OF
MARCH PAST.
Continued:

(c) The executive word of command "EYES LEFT" will be given by Platoon Commanders.

(d) Battalion Commanders and C.R.E. will fall out whilst their commands are marching past.

(e) The Divisional Band will play for the march past of the 199th Infantry Brigade Group.

(f) Should a block occur at the level crossing at S.21.b.6.4. during the march past, the nearest unit will at once be deflected into the BATAVIA CHAU. grounds.
An officer of the Brigade Staff will be in position at S.22.c.2.0. to arrange for this.

RETURN MARCH. 4. Troops will return direct to billets after marching past.

5. ACKNOWLEDGE.

R. L. Bond
Captain,
Brigade Major,
199th Infantry Brigade.

Distribution :-

Copy No. 1....Brigadier-General.
"   " 2....Brigade Major.
"   " 3....Staff Captain.
"   " 4....Brigade Signal Officer.
"   " 5....2/5th Manch.Regt.
"   " 6....2/6th   "   "
"   " 7....2/7th   "   "
"   " 8....2/8th   "   "
"   " 9....204th Machine Gun Coy.
"   " 10....199th L.T.M. Battery.
"   " 11....2/3rd Field Ambulance.
"   " 12....66th Division, "G"
"   " 13....War Diary.
"   " 14.... "   "
"   " 15....File.
"   " 16....Spare.
"   " 17.... "

DIAGRAM OF INSPECTION AND MARCH PAST.

```
                                                                        B.H.Q.                    Windmill -  ⑨  A.S.d.coy:
          2/5th L.R.    2/6th L.R.    2/7th L.R.   2/8th L.R. Sig.Sec.  L.T.P.  L.G.G.  T.M.B. → To AIRE.
  ⑨
          354ˣ          360ˣ          328ˣ         266ˣ        30ˣ      26ˣ     60ˣ      60ˣ
To ARQUES ←    ←─10ˣ─→     ←─10ˣ─→       ←─10ˣ─→      ←─75ˣ─→    ←─75ˣ─→  ←─75ˣ─→ ←─75ˣ─→

↑
Saluting Point
S.29.c.5.4. on
South side of
road.
          ←─────────────────── 1563 yards ───────────────────→
```

B. Details of Times for arrival of heads of units at S.22.c...

```
    2/3rd Field Amb.         10.5 a.m.
    204th L.A.Coy.           10.10 a.m.
    199th E.F.M.B.           10.15 a.m.
    Signal Sec. & B.H.Q.     10.20 a.m.
    2/5th March.R.           10.25 a.m.
    2/7th   "    "           10.30 a.m.
    2/6th   "    "           10.35 a.m.
    2/8th   "    "           10.40 a.m.
```

199th Infantry Brigade.   Copy No. 10.

ORDER No: 68.

Ref: Map Sheet 27.

MEDAL DISTRIBUTION. 1. The G.O.C. 66th Division will distribute medal ribbons to N.C.O.s. and men of this Brigade at 11.0 a.m. on Oct. 31st. in the main square, ARQUES.

ROUTE MARCH. 2. Units will carry out a short route march for about two hours before the parade.

DETAILS OF MEDAL DISTRIBUTION. 3. (a) The Brigade will be formed up in ARQUES square ready for the G.O.C. at 10.45 a.m.

(b) Adjutants and markers will meet the Brigade Major in the square at 10.0 a.m.

(c) Time of arrival of units in the square will be :-

  2/5th Manch.Regt.....10.15 a.m.
  2/6th   "   " .....10.20 a.m.
  2/7th   "   " .....10.25 a.m.
  2/8th   "   " .....10.30 a.m.
  L.T.M.B..............10.35 a.m.
  204th M.G.Coy........10.40 a.m.

(d) Medal recipients parade in the centre of the square at 10.30 a.m.

(e) On arrival in the square units will march on their markers, and having got their dressing will fix bayonets independently.

(f) Units will be brought to the slope by O.Cs. before the arrival of the G.O.C.

(g) On the arrival of the G.O.C. the Brigadier will give the command "General Salute, Present Arms"

(h) As their names are called out recipients of medal ribbons will march forward to the G.O.C, halt, salute, receive the ribbon, salute and return to their position in the line.

(i) Medal recipients will not proceed on the route march before parade.

DRESS. 4. (a) For medal recipients, walking out dress.
(b) For all other troops, marching order with packs. Shrapnel helmets.

RETURN TO BILLETS. 5. Units will return direct to billets on conclusion of the parade.

6. ACKNOWLEDGE.

B.H.Q.
30.10.17.

Captain,
Brigade Major,
199th Infantry Brigade.

Distribution :-

Copy No. 1....Brigadier-General.
 "   "   2....Brigade Major.
 "   "   3....Staff Captain.
 "   "   4....Brigade Signal Officer.
 "   "   5....O.C. 2/5th Manch. Regt.
 "   "   6....O.C. 2/6th   "   "
 "   "   7....O.C. 2/7th   "   "
 "   "   8....O.C. 2/8th   "   "
 "   "   9....O.C. 204th M.G.Coy.
 "   " 10....O.C. 199th L.T.M.B.
 "   " 11....66th Division, "G"
 "   " 12....66th   "   "A"
 "   " 13....A.D.C. on duty.
 "   " 14....War Diary.
 "   " 15.... "   "
 "   " 16....File.
 "   " 17....Spare.
 "   " 18.... "

Diagram to accompany Bde order No.63.

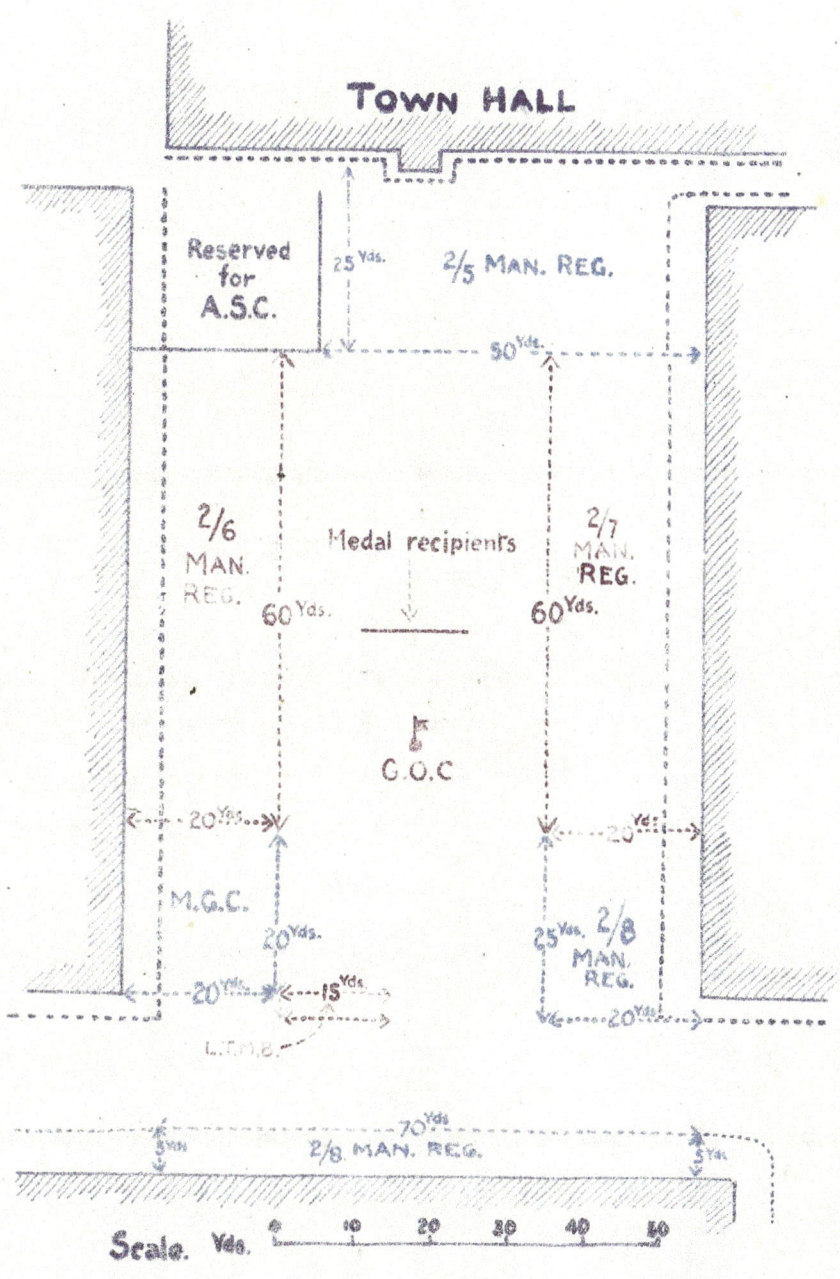

199TH B.I.

MOVING ORDER   No. 5602

1. The 49th Inf Bde Group will move to
   the WARREN-TEAPOT area tomorrow.
2. Starting point at grid ref SP 70.70
3. Route FORT ROUGE – RENESCURE –
   EBBLINGHEM
4. You will pass your starting point at
   2.36 p.m.

149 L.T.M.B.   R. [signature]
                                              Capt
                                        Adjutant 149 Inf Bde

Casualty Returns

Copy   AF W3210   Serial N°

Serial N° a/c/467   Service in France 7/12   Oct.
                                                 9
Corpl 197 KIM Bn au fem 3/5 Re inf Regt   10
                                                11
No. 20091 Rank Cpl name Hadfield S M

Age 20 Service 7/9/12   Religion Bapt

Nature of Wound Concussion

Ref   N° 4 N Z Field Ambulance

Short Summary of

Events for the Month

Army Form C. 2118.

WAR DIARY
or
INTELLIGENCE SUMMARY
(Erase heading not required.)

Instructions regarding War Diaries and Intelligence Summaries are contained in F.S. Regs., Part II. and the Staff Manual respectively. Title Pages will be prepared in manuscript.

Place	Date	Hour	Summary of Events and Information	Remarks and references to Appendices
WALLON CAPPEL	1/11/17		This month was mainly divided into two parts (i) Our stay in the YPRES sector from the 5/10/17 to 11/10/17 and (ii) our subsequent rest and training period from 14/10/17 to the end of the month. During our active service Brigade, the LTM Bty did not take an active part. From the 5/10/17 to 9/10/17 but were concentrated in reserve on HILL 40. From the 9/10/17 to the 11/10/17 I had 6 guns in the line — 3 on the right sub-section in relief of 10th Aus LTMB, 1st Aus LTMB and 3 in the left sub-section, relieving 11th LTMA. There 2 groups were situated respectively at MARVEL and HAMBURG — short distance front and north of the YPRES—ROULERS railway and east of ZONNEBEKE. On the 7th 9 withdrew the right group to H.D. POTSDAM and on the 8th the 11th Battery, including the left group, and retired to H.D. RANDOUR. On the 10th and 11th the Battery was in action. Great difficulty was experienced in taking guns into the line and bringing them out on account of the mud and water. Owing in action to the fire were monitored in shell holes and ammunition dumps close by. Ammunition supply was also very difficult and supplied to left group about 250 rounds which were being covered over by Tarpaulines, and the right group into 100 rounds which I found at BEECHAM and the right group carried in got up from the main dumps. On the night of 7th my left group was ordered in support of a counter-attack — disposing of ammunition. No ammunition was in attempting a counter attack — disposing fuzes, the enemy who were concentrating in the Cemetery and Augustus Wood, luckily in Cavalry in extreme to lay anything down to retrieve. We were interested to bring the guns to action by above was very effective in this type of situation found that a machine

Army Form C. 2118.

WAR DIARY
or
INTELLIGENCE SUMMARY

(Erase heading not required.)

Instructions regarding War Diaries and Intelligence Summaries are contained in F. S. Regs., Part II. and the Staff Manual respectively. Title Pages will be prepared in manuscript.

Place	Date	Hour	Summary of Events and Information	Remarks and references to Appendices
			From the 19/10/17 to the end of the month we rested and training in the ARQUES area during which we practised formations & carried the guns pants with slings and giving infantry the apperature. This method we found very effective, and intend to use it in action next time. The weather throughout the month was unsettled.	

Julia Whiriley Capt.
O.C. 199th MGC

Army Form W.3091.

Cover for Documents.

CONFIDENTIAL

Nature of Enclosures.

WAR DIARY
OF
199th L.T.M. B'ty.
FROM
1st NOV — 30th NOV 1917

VOLUME V

Notes, or Letters written.

APPENDIX
I OPERATION ORDERS
II SUMMARY OF EVENTS
III CASUALTY RETURNS

WAR DIARY
or
INTELLIGENCE SUMMARY

(Erase heading not required.)

Army Form C. 2118.

Instructions regarding War Diaries and Intelligence Summaries are contained in F. S. Regs., Part II. and the Staff Manual respectively. Title Pages will be prepared in manuscript.

Place	Date	Hour	Summary of Events and Information	Remarks and references to Appendices
ARQUES	1917 Nov 1st		Weather wet. Received B.O.O. No. 10-64 & 6/M/No.-10. Commn. sheets Nos. no-33. The Battn marched out & Billets in accordance with B.O.O. No. 64 marching thro' to ARQUES to STAPLES arriving at camp at about 6-45 S&q.	B.O.O No. 10-64
STAPLE	"2		Weather fine. Training. S&q	
"	"3		Weather unsettled. Training. S&q	
"	"4		Weather fine. Training. S&q	
"	"5		Weather unsettled. Training. S&q	
"	"6		Weather wet. The Battn took part in a Brigade Scheme taken near Pte: ta village. Guns carried by slings & no leg used. Invited Warning Order no-3 S&q	Warning Order no-3 W.O.B. No. 24
"	"7		Weather wet. Training. Received Commn. sheet week no 24 also Commn. Order no. 24. S&q	

WAR DIARY
or
INTELLIGENCE SUMMARY

(Erase heading not required.)

Army Form C. 2118.

Place	Date	Hour	Summary of Events and Information	Remarks and references to Appendices
STAPLE	1917 Nov 8th		Weather wet. Training packing. Received B.O.O. no - 65 B. by no. 10. Administration Order no - 25	B.O.O. no 65 Admin no 25
"	" 9th		Weather wet. The Battery moved in accordance with B.O.O. no - 15. The Battery marched to EBBLINGHEN Station where it entrained, detraining at CAUDERDON. We then marched into a camp in the WESTOUTRE area. Received B.O.O. no. 66 & by no. 19 also Administration Order no. 26	B.O.O. no 66 Admin no. 26
WESTOUTRE AREA A. "10"			Weather wet. The Battery moved in accordance with B.O.O.no.66. Leaving camp about 9 a.m marching via RENINGHELST - LEVECOTEN - HALLEBAST - DICKIE BUSH to detachment near BELGIAN BATTERY CORNER, where we arrived about 12-30 p.m. 1 O.R. casualty.	S.e.q
CANAL AREA YPRES "11"			Weather wet. Training. Building cook houses &c.	S.e.q

Army Form C. 2118.

WAR DIARY
or
INTELLIGENCE SUMMARY
(Erase heading not required.)

Instructions regarding War Diaries and Intelligence Summaries are contained in F. S. Regs., Part II. and the Staff Manual respectively. Title Pages will be prepared in manuscript.

Place	Date	Hour	Summary of Events and Information	Remarks and references to Appendices
CANAL AREA	May 1917 12th		Weather fair. Training. S69	
YPRES	13th		Weather fair. Training S69	
"	14th		Weather fair. Training S69	
"	15th		Weather fair Training S69	
"	16th		Weather unsettled. Training.	
"	17th		Weather fine. Received B.O.O no 67 para 1-10. S69	Training orders
"	18th		Weather fine. Received B.O.O no 67 para 11-14 S69	3.0.0. no 67
"	19th		Weather fine. Church parade &c. Received Addendum to B.O.O no 67 para No 14. Also addendum to administration order on B.O.O no 67. Also addendum to B.O.O no 67. S69	addendum to B.0.0 67 addendum Admin Order to B.O. 67

Army Form C. 2118.

WAR DIARY
or
INTELLIGENCE SUMMARY

(Erase heading not required.)

Instructions regarding War Diaries and Intelligence Summaries are contained in F. S. Regs., Part II. and the Staff Manual respectively. Title Pages will be prepared in manuscript.

Place	Date	Hour	Summary of Events and Information	Remarks and references to Appendices
CANAL AREA YPRES.	1917 Nov 19		Weather fine. Training S.O.S	
ESPLANADE S.A.P. YPRES	Nov 20		Battery moved out of canal area to Esplanade Sap, Ypres at 12 noon. Battery arrived Esplanade Sap at 12.30 p.m. and relieved 197th L.T.M.B. Enemy shelled in the vicinity of Esplanade Sap about 9 p.m. Weather dull. Some training carried out.	B.O. 70 68 addendum
"	Nov 21		Received B.O. No 68 and addendum to B.O. No 68. Some training out during the day. Weather fine.	to B.O. No 68
MONTREAL CAMP OUDERDOM.	Nov 22		Moved out of YPRES at 11.30 A.M. and arrived MONTREAL CAMP at 2 P.M. Weather fine.	
"	Nov 23		Received B.O. 69 and administration Order No 30. Weather dull. Some training carried out during the day. Received addendum to B.O. 69	B.O. 69 A.O. 30 addendum to B.O. 69
BERTHEN AREA	Nov 24		Battery moved independently from MONTREAL CAMP and arrived BERTHEN. Weather fine at 12 noon.	
"	Nov 25		Weather fine. Training S.O.S Received B.O. 70 and A.O. 31 also A.O. 31 and A.O. 32.	B.O. 70 A.O. 31 A.O. 32

Army Form C. 2118.

WAR DIARY
or
INTELLIGENCE SUMMARY

(Erase heading not required.)

Instructions regarding War Diaries and Intelligence Summaries are contained in F. S. Regs., Part II. and the Staff Manual respectively. Title Pages will be prepared in manuscript.

Place	Date	Hour	Summary of Events and Information	Remarks and references to Appendices
STAPLE SUB-AREA No 2 (EASTERN)	Nov 26/17		Battery moved independently from BERTHEN and arrived at STAPLE AREA at 1 P.M. H.Q. fixed at P 36 a 7.7. (sheet 27). Weather fine.	
—	Nov 27		Weather fine. Training	
—	Nov 28		Weather dull. Training	
—	Nov 29		Weather dull. Training	
—	Nov 30		Weather dull. Training	

[signature]
O.C. 199th L.T.M.B.

APPENDIX

I

OPERATION

ORDERS

SECRET.   Copy No. 10.

199th Infantry Brigade
ORDER No: 64.

Ref: Map Sheet 27. 1/40,000.

1. The 199th Infantry Brigade Group will move to the WALLON-CAPPEL area (STAPLE Sub-area) on Nov.1st.1917.

2. A march table is attached.

3. Distances laid down in 66th Div. 520/1 G. 29.9.17, this Office No.G.466, 29.9.17. will be maintained on the march.

4. Officers and men belonging to Brigade Reinforcement School will move with their own units, and the School will be reopened in the new area under instructions which will be issued later.

5. Administrative instructions are being issued separately.

6. Brigade Headquarters will close at ARQUES at 1.30 p.m. and reopen at STAPLE at the same hour.

7. Units should take with them all training material in their possession, and not leave any dumped at ARQUES.

8. ACKNOWLEDGE.

R. W. Bond
Captain,
Brigade Major,
199th Infantry Brigade.

31.10.17.

Distribution :-

```
Copy No. 1....Brigadier-General.
 "    "  2....Brigade Major.
 "    "  3....Staff Captain.
 "    "  4....Brigade Signal Officer.
 "    "  5....2/5th Manch. Regt.
 "    "  6....2/6th   "     "
 "    "  7....2/7th   "     "
 "    "  8....2/8th   "     "
 "    "  9....204th M.G.Coy.
 "    " 10....199th L.T.M.B.
 "    " 11....Bde. Reinforcement School.
 "    " 12....66th Division, "G"
 "    " 13....66th    "      "A"
 "    " 14....2/3rd Field Ambulance.
 "    " 15....544 Coy. A.S.C.
 "    " 16....War Diary.
 "    " 17....  "    "
 "    " 18....File.
 "    " 19....Spare.
 "    " 20....  "
```

MARCH TABLE TO ACCOMPANY 199th
Infantry Brigade ORDER NO:64.

UNIT. In order of March.	Starting Point.	Time of passing S.P.	Route.	Destination.	REMARKS.
Bde.H.Q. and Signal Section.	Rd.junct.S.17.c.70.75.	1.32 p.m.	FORT ROUGE-Rd.Junc.T.10.c.0.7. -Cross Roads T.10.c.3.2. - STAPLE.	STAPLE. area.	Moves independently in the morning about 11 a.m.
2/5th Manch.R.	"	1.32 p.m.		"	Guides from billeting parties to meet units at rd. junct. T.11.d.7.7. at 2.45 p.m.
2/7th Manch.R.	"	2.0 p.m.		"	"
2/8th Manch.R.	"	2.13 p.m.		"	"
199 L.T.M.B.	"	2.36 p.m.		"	Cyclist guide from battalion party will be provided.
204th M.G.Coy.	"	2.40 p.m.		"	"
2/3rd Fld.Amb.	"	2.45 p.m.		"	"
2/6th Manch.R.	Rd.junc.S.22.c.3.5.	2.07 p.m.	CAMPAGNE- RENESCURE- X rds. U.19. a.6.2.	"	Moves independently. Guide to meet Battalion at X roads U.19.a.6.2.
544 Coy A.S.C.				"	Moves independently in the morning.

SECRET.   Copy No. 14

199th Infantry Brigade
ADMINISTRATIVE ORDER
No:23.

Ref: 199th Bde. Operation Order No.64.
Ref: Maps BELGIUM & FRANCE.
 Sheet 27, 1/40,000.

TRANSPORT. 1. First line transport will accompany units.
The 544 Coy. A.S.C. will move independently and will be met by guides at T.11.d.8.7. at 12 noon.
Second line baggage wagons will report at Q.M.Stores of 2/6th Manch.R. at 7 a.m. and of other units at 7.30 am. They will march with the Train Coy. and be formed into a convoy on ARQUES-HAZEBROUCK road at road junction in S.17.c.75.70 by 10 a.m.

LORRIES. 2. Seven lorries have been allotted to the Brigade Group for the purpose of carrying blankets, surplus kits, stores etc. These lorries will each make two journeys. For the first journey lorries are allotted as follows :-

```
         Bde. H.Qrs.       1 lorry.         No.1.
         2/5th Manch.R.    1   "             "  2.
         2/6th   "    "    1   "             "  3.
         2/7th   "    "    1   "             "  4.
         2/8th   "    "    1   "             "  5.
         L.T.M.B.          1   "             "  6.
         204th M.G.Coy.    1   "             "  7.
```

The above units will send guides to the square, ARQUES, at 8 a.m. to conduct lorries to their Q.M.Stores. An unloading party of an N.C.O. and four men will accompany each lorry. The lorries will proceed as a convoy to Area Commandant's Office, STAPLE.
N.C.O.s. in charge of lorries will report to an officer of Brigade Headquarters at road junction in S.17.c.75.70 at 10.30 a.m.
For the second journey lorries are allotted as follows :-

```
         2/5th Manch.R.    1 lorry.         No.1.
         2/5th   "    "    1   "             "  2.
         2/6th   "    "    1   "             "  3.
         2/7th   "    "    1   "             "  4.
         2/8th   "    "    1   "             "  5.
         2/6th   "    "    1   "             "  6.
         2/3rd Fld.Amb.    1   "             "  7.
```

The 2/3rd Field Ambulance will have a guide in the square at ARQUES at 2 p.m. to conduct lorry to their Q.M.Stores.

RATIONS. 3. Representatives of units will attend at Refilling Point at 8 a.m. tomorrow Nov.1st.
Rations for consumption of Nov.2nd. will be loaded on to train wagons and delivered to units on arrival in new area.

(-2-).

BILLETING PARTIES. 4. A bus has been placed at the disposal of the Brigade Group for billeting parties. Seats are allotted as follows:

        Brigade H.Q.   2.
        2/5th Manch.R. 4.
        2/6th " "   4.
        2/7th " "   4.
        2/8th " "   4.
        204th M.G.C.   2.
        L.T.M.B.   2.
        544 Coy.A.S.C. 3.
                      25.

The above parties will report to the Staff Captain at Brigade Headquarters at 6 a.m.
In addition to the above, units will send a party of at least an N.C.O. and four men on cycles to report to Staff Captain at Brigade Headquarters at 7.15 a.m. The 2/5th Manch.R. will detail an officer to take charge of this party, which will proceed to Area Commandant's Office, STAPLE and await the arrival of the remainder of the billeting party.

BILLETS. 5. The Brigadier-General hopes that all units will leave their billets and transport lines in the same clean and satisfactory condition as has always been the case in this Brigade.

6. ACKNOWLEDGE.

                                  Captain,
                              Staff Captain,
31.10.17.   199th Infantry Brigade.

Distribution :-

Copy No. 1...Brigadier-General.
" " 2...Brigade Major.
" " 3...Staff Captain.
" " 4...Brigade Signal Officer.
" " 5...2/5th Manch.Regt.
" " 6...2/6th " "
" " 7...2/7th " "
" " 8...2/8th " "
" " 9...Q.M. 2/5th Manch.R.
" " 10...Q.M. 2/6th " "
" " 11...Q.M. 2/7th " "
" " 12...Q.M. 2/8th " "
" " 13...204th M.G.Coy.
" " 14...199th L.T.M.Battery.
" " 15...Bde.Reinforcement School.
" " 16...66th Division, "G"
" " 17...66th " "A"
" " 18...2/3rd Field Amb.
" " 19...544 Coy. A.S.C.
" " 20...War Diary.
" " 21..." "
" " 22...File.
" " 23...Spare.
" " 24..."
" " 25...O.C. Divnl. Train.

199 L.T.M.B.

199th Infantry Brigade Group
Administrative Order No. 24

Reference Maps BELGIUM & FRANCE Sheets 27 & 28.
1/40,000

TRANSPORT. 1. The Transport of the 199th Infantry Brigade Group will move from STAPLE to EECKE on the 8th inst. and to RENINGHELST Area on the 9th instant.

Regimental Transport will be under the command of Lieut THORNE (A.S.C. Mane. R.) who will act as Brigade Transport Officer to the Transport other than 544 Coy ASC.

STARTING POINT. 2. The Starting Point will be the Cross Roads at LONGUECROIX (V 5 c 3.4) Ref Sheet 27

ROUTE 3. Cross Roads LA BREARDE V 5 c 4.1 — Cross Roads P 30 a 1.3 — Road Junction Q 20 c 9.7 — Billets

ROUTE in EECKE area.
(continued) On second day CAESTRE - BAILLEUL - LOCRE - WESTOUTRE - RENINGHELST Area.

TIME OF STARTING :- Units Transport will pass Starting Point at the following Times on the 8th inst. :-

544 Coy A.S.C.   11 a.m
2/8th Manch R.   11-15 am
2/7th   "   "   11-20 "
2/5th   "   "   11-25 "
2/6th   "   "   11-30 "
204 M.G Coy.   11-35 "
199 B. HQ   11-40 "
2/3rd field Amb.   11-45 "

On the 9th inst., Transport will be clear of

Page 3

EECKE by 8 a.m.
Orders for place and time of starting will be issued by senior Officer.

DISTANCES 5. Distances as laid down in 199 Inf. Bde. G.466 of 20-9-17 are to be observed on the march. The 544 Coy A.S.C. will march at least 1000 yards ahead of the Regimental Transport.

ADVANCE PARTY FOR TRANSPORT 6. Two mounted orderlies will be detailed by each Unit as billeting party for transport. They will report to Officer to be detailed by 2/8 Worcester Regt at Cross Roads LONGUE CROIX (U 5 c 3.4) at 9 a.m. on the 8th inst.

Billets will be allotted for the night of the 8th/9th on application to the Area Commandant EECKE.
Guides for advance

Page 4

ADVANCE PARTY (cont'd) party will meet the Transport at road junction O.20.c.9.7 at 2 p.m. on the 8th inst.

On arrival in RENINGHELST area on the 9th inst, the Brigade Transport Officer will report at Batt. H.Q. the position of which will be notified to him before departure on the 8th.

TRAIN WAGONS 7. The Train Wagons will be sent to thirds at 7.30 a.m. on the 8th inst. and will move with 1st Line Transport to EECKE where they will join the 5th Coy A.S.C. under arrangements to be made by the O.C. 5th Coy A.S.C. and the Brigade Transport Officer.

RATIONS 8. The unexpended portion of the rations for the 8th inst. and rations for the 9th will be taken with the Transport.

POSITION 9. Officers Commanding will take steps to ensure that their transport debouches on to the road in its correct

Page 5

position as regards other Units

MARCH DISCIPLINE 10. Particular attention is to be paid to March discipline.

LOADING OF TRANSPORT 11. The state of the roads calls for the greatest care in the loading of Transport. Commanding Officers will be held responsible that wagons are not overloaded.

A Staff Officer will be detailed to inspect the column on the march, to note that the loading has been properly carried out and that loads are not excessive.

MAPS 12. Units will ensure that their Transport Officers are provided with the necessary maps.

MOBILE VETERINARY SECTION 13. The 1/1st E.L. Mobile Veterinary Section will be attached to the 8th Div. and will move with the 54th Coy A.S.C. The O.C. 54th Coy A.S.C. will make the necessary arrangements for billets &c.

Page 6.

LORRIES 14. See this Office Wire P.7. of the 7th inst. Detailed instructions as to guides and loading parties will be issued later.

BILLETING PARTY 15. A Bus will leave Brigade H.Q. for RENINGHELST at 8-30 a.m. on the 8th inst.

The following parties will be detailed by units and will report at the Bde. H.Q. at 8-15 a.m. to the Staff Captain.

Each Battalion — 4
204 M.G. Coy. — 2
199 L.T.M.B. — 2
54th Coy A.S.C. — 2
Brigade Headquarters — 2

16. ACKNOWLEDGE

B.H.Q.
7-11-17

[signature] Captain
Staff Captain
199th Infantry Brigade

199th Infantry Brigade

Addendum to Administrative Order No 24

BILLETS. 1. The Billets for the 9th inst. will be allotted to Units by Area Commandant, WESTOUTRE. The location cannot yet be notified of the area to be allotted to the Brigade Group.
It will not be the RENINGHELST Area.

TRANSPORT. 2. The billets for the Transport for the night of 8th–9th inst will be allotted by the Area Commandant, EECKE as already notified.
The billets will however probably be at GODEWAERSVELDE.

ROUTE 3. If the Transport is billeted at GODEWAERSVELDE, the route laid down in para. 3 of the above Brigade Order will not be adhered to. The Senior Officer will arrange with the Brigade Transport Officer to have the more direct routes to WESTOUTRE

Page 2

ROUTE reconnoitred in
(continued) advance and will issue
orders accordingly

ADVANCE PARTY 4. He will also detail
an advance party to
report to Area Commandant
WESTOUTRE, who will
allot billets for the Transport
for the 9th inst.

GUIDES 5. He will issue orders
for Guides from Advance
Party to meet Transport
at least a mile outside
WESTOUTRE.

6. ACKNOWLEDGE.

B.H.Q
8-11-17

Wrath Unsworth
Captain
Staff Captain
199th Infantry Brigade

SECRET.   199TH. INFANTRY BRIGADE GROUP.   Copy No. 10

ADMINISTRATIVE ORDER No. 25.

Reference:- 199th. Operation Order No. 65.

LORRIES. 1. Seven Lorries have been allotted to the Brigade Group for the purpose of carrying the remaining Stores, cooking utensils, etc. which are not being carried on the Transport. One blanket per man is also to be carried on lorries. These lorries will each make two journeys.

They are allotted as follows :-

Brigade Headquarters.	1 Lorry.
2/5th. Manch. Regt.	1 "
2/6th. " "	1 "
2/7th. " "	1 "
2/8th. " "	1 "
L.T.M.B.	1 "
204th. M.G.Coy.) 2/3rd. Field. Amb.)	1 "
	7 Lorries.

The lorry allotted to the 204 M.G.Coy. will return for the stores of the 2/3rd. Field. Amb.
The above units will send guides to Bde. H.Q. at 7-45 a.m. on the 9th. inst. to conduct lorries to their Q.M.Stores.
An unloading party of an N.C.O. and 4 men will accompany each lorry.
N.C.Os. in charge of lorries will report to an Officer to be detailed by Brigade, at Cross Roads LONGUE CROIX, U.5.c 3.4 at 10 a.m. Lorries will proceed from this point as a convoy to the Area Commandant's Office, WESTOUTRE, where they will be met by guides from the advanced billeting party. Every effort should be made to get the lorries unloaded and returned without undue delay.

BLANKETS. 2. One blanket will be carried on the man.

RATIONS. 3. Rations for the 10th. will be delivered to Units by train wagons on the 9th. inst. in the WESTOUTRE Area.

GUIDES. 4. Guides from the advanced billeting parties will meet units at the Station OUDERDAM at the following times :-

Brigade Headquarters.	9-45 a.m.
2/5th. Manch. Regt.	" "
2/6th. " "	" "
204th. M.G. Coy.	" "
199th. L.T.M.B.	" "
2/7th. Manch. Regt.	5-0. p.m.
2/8th. " "	" "
2/3rd. Field. Amb.	" "

7. ACKNOWLEDGE.

B.H.Q.
8-11-17.

Captain.
Staff Captain.
199th. Infantry Brigade.

Distribution:-

Copy No. 1. Brigadier-General.
" 2. Brigade Major.
3. Staff Captain.
4. Brigade Signal Officer.
5. 2/5th. Manchester Regt.
6. 2/6th. " "
7. 2/7th. " "
8. 2/8th. " "
9. 204th. Machine Gun Coy.
10. 199th. L.T.M.B.
11. 432nd. Field Coy. R.E.
12. 2/3rd. Field Ambulance.
13. 66th. Division. "G".
14. 66th. Division. "Q".
15. C. R. E.
16.
17. War Diary.
18. " "
19. File.
20. Spare.
21.
22.
23.
24. C.S.O.

SECRET.   Copy No. 14

199th Infantry Brigade
ADMINISTRATIVE ORDER NO. 26.

Ref. 199th Infantry Brigade ORDER No. 66.

TRANSPORT. 1. The 1st line transport will accompany units on march from WESTOUTRE Area to BELGIAN CHATEAU.

2. The Train Baggage Waggons will remain with units for the night of the 9th/10th, and move with 1st line transport. The O.C. 544 Coy. A.S.C. will arrange for the horses for Train wagons to be sent to units transport lines before 7.30 a.m. A baggage wagon will be provided for L.T.M.B.

3. Distances as laid down in 199th Infantry Brigade Order G.46 of 29.9.17. will be adhered to.

LORRIES. 4. Six lorries have been allotted to the Brigade for the purpose of carrying two blankets per man, stores etc. These lorries will each make two journeys.
Lorries are allotted as follows :-

	1st Journey.	2nd Journey.
No. 1.	B.H.Q.	B.H.Q. & L.T.M.B.
" 2.	2/5th M.R.	2/5th M.R.
" 3.	2/5th M.R.	2/6th M.R.
" 4.	2/6th M.R.	2/6th M.R.
" 5.	2/7th M.R.	2/7th M.R.
" 6.	M.G.Coy.	2/7th M.R.

The above units will send guides to fork roads HEKSKEN M.3.c.1.3. at 7 a.m. tomorrow 10th inst. to conduct lorries to Q.M.Stores.
2/6th and 2/7th Manch.Regt. will detail guides to accompany lorries Nos. 3 & 6 respectively on first journey and conduct them to their Q.M.Stores on their return journey.
The lorries will assemble at the above fork roads at 9 a.m. and proceed as a convoy to BELGIAN BATTERY corner H.24.a.3.8.
An unloading party of one N.C.O. and four men will accompany each lorry. This number must not be exceeded.
Officers in charge of advanced billeting parties will detail guides to be at above point at 10 a.m. to conduct lorries to Q.M.Stores in new area.
A lorry will bring the remaining stores of L.T.M.B. left in STAPLE Area to BELGIAN BATTERY corner direct.
O.C. L.T.M.B. will detail a guide to be at this point at 9 a.m.

RATIONS. 5. Rations for the 11th. will be delivered to units on arrival in new area on the 10th. Units will detail guides to meet supply waggons at BELGIAN BATTERY corner at 2 p.m. on the 10th. The rations for the 2/8th Manch.R. will be delivered to their present Q.M.Stores.

(-2-).

BILLETING PARTY. 6. Units will detail an advanced billeting party to meet Lieut. TURPIN at Area Commandant's Office, BELGIAN CHATEAU, H.23.b.3.7. at 9 a.m. tomorrow 10th inst.

GUIDES. 7. Guides will be detailed from advanced parties to meet units at BELGIAN BATTERY corner at 10.30 a.m. Guides will also be provided to meet lorries as detailed above.

BLANKETS. 8. Blankets will not be carried on the man.

                                                            Captain,
                                              Staff Captain,
B.H.Q.   199th Infantry Brigade.
9.11.17.

Distribution.

Copy No. 1...Brigadier-General.
"   "   2...Brigade Major.
"   "   3...Staff Captain.
"   "   4...Brigade Signal Officer.
"   "   5...2/5th Manch.R.
"   "   6...2/6th   "   "
"   "   7...2/7th   "   "
"   "   8...2/8th   "   "
"   "   9...Q.M. 2/5th Manch.R.
"   "   10...Q.M. 2/6th   "   "
"   "   11...Q.M. 2/7th   "   "
"   "   12...Q.M. 2/8th   "   "
"   "   13...204th Machine Gun Coy.
"   "   14...199th L.T.M. Battery.
"   "   15...544 Coy. A.S.C.
"   "   16...66th Divisional Train.
"   "   17...66th Division, "G"
"   "   18...66th   "   "Q"
"   "   19...S.S.C. 66th Division.
"   "   20...1st Australian Div.
"   "   21...2nd Australian Inf.Bde.
"   "   22...War Diary.
"   "   23..." "
"   "   24...File.
"   "   25...Spare.
"   "   26..."

SECRET.   Copy No...14

Addendum to 199th Infantry Brigade ORDER No.67.

LORRIES.   1. The following Lorries are allotted to units for move on 20th inst.

                 2/5th Manch.R......1 lorry.
                 2/6th " " ......1 "
                 2/7th " " ......1 "
                 L.T.M.B............1 "
                 Bde.H.Q............1 "

These lorries will make two or more journeys as required.
2/5th Manch.Regt. will detail an officer to meet the lorries at BELGIAN BATTERY CORNER, H.24.a.4.8. at 8 a.m. on 20th inst. who will allot the lorries to guides detailed by above units.

RATIONS.   2. Rations for 2/5th, 2/6th, 2/7th Manch.Regt. L.T.M.B. and 199th Bde. H.Q. will be delivered to Q.M.Stores by train wagons on the 20th inst. for consumption on 21st.

BAGGAGE WAGONS.   3. No train wagons for conveyance of baggage will be available on 20th inst.

                                                 Captain,
                                                 Staff Captain,
    18.11.17.   199th Infantry Brigade.

Distribution :-

Copy No.1....Brigadier-General.
"   " 2....Brigade Major.
"   " 3....Staff Captain.
"   " 4....Bde. Signal Officer.
"   " 5....2/5th Manch.Regt.
"   " 6....2/6th "   "
"   " 7....2/7th "   "
"   " 8....2/8th "   "
"   " 9....Q.M. 2/5th Manch.Regt.
"   "10....Q.M. 2/6th "   "
"   "11....Q.M. 2/7th "   "
"   "12....Q.M. 2/8th "   "
"   "13....204th M.G.Coy.
"   "14....199th L.T.M.B.
"   "15....544 Coy. A.S.C.
"   "16....197th Inf. Bde.
"   "17.... "   "   "
"   "18....198th "   "
"   "19....66th Division, "G"
"   "20....66th   "   "Q"
"   "21....Area Commandant, CANAL AREA.
"   "22....War Diary.
"   "23.... "
"   "24....File.
"   "25....Spare.
"   "26....
"   "27.... 66 Div Train

SECRET.   Copy No. 10

        Addendum to 199th Infantry Brigade
             Order No. 67.

                                                                    ON. Nov. 20th

1.   Brigade Headquarters will close at CHAU BELGE at 11.0 a.m.
     and re-open at Infantry Barracks YPRES at the same hour.

2.   The 2/8th Manchester Regiment after relieving 2/4th
     East Lancs. Regiment will be at the tactical disposal
     of G.O.C. Brigade in the Line.
     The senior O.C. of the two Companies to be accommodated
     in RAILWAY WOOD dug-outs will report personally to
     Brigade Headquarters at D.26.c.1.3. after relief, and
     will arrange to have two runners permanently at these
     Headquarters.

3(a) Brigade Order No. 67, para. 3a, after "Company" add
     "and 9th Army Tramway Company".
 (b) Brigade Order No. 67, para, 3b, is cancelled. The
     Companies of the 2/7th Manchester Regiment working under
     145 Army Troops   Company, R.E., will be relieved
     at 10-30 am. on November 19th by a Unit of 1st New
     Zealand Brigade. Details of Guides etc., will be notified
     later to O.C. 2/7th Manchester Regiment.

4.   Completion of all reliefs to be reported to Brigade Head-
     quarters by code word "SOCKS".

5.   ACKNOWLEDGE.

                                                    Captain.
                                                    Brigade Major.
18.11.17.   199th Infantry Brigade.

     DISTRIBUTION.

     Copy No. 1.......Brigadier-General.
             2.......Brigade Major.
             3.......Staff Captain.
             4.......Brigade Signal Officer
             5.......2/5th Manch. Regiment.
             6.......2/6th   "   "
             7.......2/7th   "   "
             8.......2/8th   "   "
             9.......204th M.G. Company
            10.......199th L.T.M. Battery.
            11.......544 Coy A.S.C.
            12.......197th Infantry Brigade.
            13....... "   "   "
            14.......198th   "   "
            15.......66th Division "G"
            16.......66th   "   "Q"
            17.......Area Commandant, CANAL Area.
            18.......)War Diary.
            19.......)
            20.......File.
            21.......Spare.
            22....... "

SECRET.   Copy No. 14

Addendum to 199th Infantry Brigade ORDER No: 67.

TRANSPORT LINES. 1. The Transport lines of B.H.Q, 2/5th, 2/6th, 2/7th Bns. Manch.Regt. and 204th Machine Gun Coy. will remain as at present when the Brigade moves into YPRES
2/8th Bn Manch.Regt. will take over transport lines and Q.M.Stores of the 2/7th Lanc.Fslrs. on the 19th inst.
The Commanding Officer of 2/8th Manch.Regt. will get into touch with his opposite number of 197th Infantry Brigade and will make all arrangements for taking over the lines with the unit concerned direct.

RATIONS. 2. Rations will continue to be drawn by regimental transport from refilling point when units move to new area.

3. ACKNOWLEDGE.

Gerald Unsworth
Captain,
Staff Captain,
199th Infantry Brigade.

18.11.17.

Distribution:-

Copy No. 1...Brigadier-General.
 "   "   2...Brigade Major.
 "   "   3...Staff Captain.
 "   "   4...Bde.Signal Officer.
 "   "   5...2/5th Manch.Regt.
 "   "   6...2/6th   "   "
 "   "   7...2/7th   "   "
 "   "   8...2/8th   "   "
 "   "   9...Q.M. 2/5th Manch.Regt.
 "   " 10...Q.M. 2/6th   "   "
 "   " 11...Q.M. 2/7th   "   "
 "   " 12...Q.M. 2/8th   "   "
 "   " 13...204th M.G.Coy.
 "   " 14...199th L.T.M.B.
 "   " 15...544 Coy. A.S.C.
 "   " 16...197th Inf. Bde.
 "   " 17...   "   "   "
 "   " 18...198th   "   "
 "   " 19...66th Division, "G"
 "   " 20...66th   "   "Q"
 "   " 21...Area Commandant, CANAL AREA.
 "   " 22...War Diary.
 "   " 23...   "   "
 "   " 24...File.
 "   " 25...Spare.
 "   " 26...

SECRET.   Copy No. 9

Addendum to 199th Infantry Brigade Order No. 68.

BILLETS.	1.	The 2/5th, 2/6th, and 2/7th Manchester Regiment will take over Billets in CANAL Area vacated by the 197th Inf; Brigade. The 2/8th Manchester Regiment will take over the Billets vacated by the 2/7th Lancashire Fusiliers in MONTREAL CAMP. By arrangements with O.C. 2/8th Manchester Regiment the 199th Brigade L.T.M.Battery will also be billetted in MONTREAL CAMP.
TRANSPORT LINES.	2.	The Transport Lines and Quarter-masters Stores of the 2/5th, 2/6th and 2/7th Manchester Regiments will remain as at present. The 2/8th Manchester Regiment will take over the Transport lines in MONTREAL CAMP vacated by the 2/7th Lancs; Fusiliers.
LORRIES.	3.	The following lorries are allotted for the move on the 22nd November :-

```
                B'de Hdqrs........1 Lorry.
                2/5th Manch.Regt. 2  "
                2/6th   "    "    2  "
                2/7th   "    "    2  "
                2/8th   "    "    2  "
                L.T.M.B...........1  "
```

Two lorries will report at Headquarters 2/6th Manchester Regiment (I.13.c.4.9.) at 8-0 a.m.
The remaining 8 lorries will report to an Officer to be detailed by the 2/8th Manchester Regiment at the INFANTRY BARRACKS at 8-0 a.m.
The lorries will be allotted to Guides to be detailed by the above Units. All lorries to be clear of BELGIAN BATTERY CORNER by 9-45 a.m.

TRAIN WAGONS.	4.	No Train Wagons for conveyance of Baggage will be available for move on 22nd instant.
RATIONS.	5.	Units will continue to draw rations from Refilling Point with Regimental Transport. The 2/8th Manchester Regiment will arrange to draw Rations for L.T.M.Battery.
	6.	ACKNOWLEDGE.

                                                Captain.
                                   Staff Captain.
                         199th Infantry Brigade.

B.H.Q.
21.11.17.

DISTRIBUTION.

```
Copy No......1. Brigadier-General.
             2.  Brigade Major.
             3.  Staff Captain.
             4.  O.C. 2/5th Manchesters.
             5.   "   2/6th      "
             6.   "   2/7th      "
             7.   "   2/8th      "
             8.   "   204th M.G.Company.
             9.   "   199th L.T.M.Battery.
            10.  Q.M. 2/5th Manchesters.
            11.   "   2/6th      "
            12.   "   2/7th      "
            13.   "   2/8th      "
            14.  66th Division "G"
            15.   "      "     "Q"
            16.  S.S.C. 66th Division.
            17.  S.C. 199th Brigade.
            18.  544 Coy A.S.C.
            19.  197th Inf. Brigade.
            20.  198th  "      "
            21.  C.R.E.
            22.  A.D.M.S.
            23.  2/3rd Field Ambulance.
            24.  202nd M.G.Coy.
            25.  )
            26.  ) War Diary.
            27, 28, Spare.
```

SECRET.   Copy No. 13

                                                          22.11.17.

                        199th Infantry Brigade
                        ADMINISTRATION ORDER NO.
                                 30.

Ref: 199th Infantry Brigade Order No.69.

Ref: Sheets 27 & 28, BELGIUM & FRANCE 1/40.000.

1. BILLETS.

   On the 24th inst. the 199th Infantry Brigade Group will move into billets in the BERTHEN AREA (less the 204th Machine Gun Coy. and 8 guns 202nd Machine Gun Coy. which will move into this area on the 25th inst. Billets will be allotted on application to the Area Commandant, BERTHEN.
   The following is the approximate position of the billeting areas to be occupied by the undermentioned units :-

Unit	Location	Map Ref	
Bde.H.Q.	BERTHEN.	R.22.c.6.8.	
2/5th Manch.R.		R.32.b. & d	and R.32.a & c.
2/6th " "		R.33.b & d.	" R.24.a & c.
2/7th " "		R.27.b & d.	" R.28.a & c.
2/8th " "		X.1.a.	
204th M.G.Coy.		X.8.d.	
199th L.T.M.B.		R.21.a.5.5.	
544 Coy. A.S.C.		X.4.c.	

2. ADVANCE BILLETING PARTIES.

   The following billeting parties will be detailed by the undermentioned units :-

Unit	Officers	Interpreter	O.R's
Bde.H.Q.	1 Off.	1 Interpreter,	4 O.R's.
2/5th Manch.R.	1 Offr.	1 Intptr.	6 O.R's.
2/6th " "	1 "	Nil.	6 "
2/7th " "	1 "	"	6 "
2/8th " "	1 "	1 Intpr.	6 "
199th L.T.M.B.	1 "	Nil.	2 "
544 Coy. A.S.C.	1 "	"	2 "
204th M.G.Coy.	1 "	"	2 "
202nd " "	1 "	1 Intpr.	2 "
	9. "	4 "	36

   The parties detailed by Brigade Headquarters, 2/5th, 2/6th, 2/7th Bn Manch.Regt. and 204th and 202nd M.G.Coys. will embus at Brigade Headquarters, BELGIAN CHATEAU at 8 a.m. on the 23rd inst.
   The parties from 2/8th Manch.Regt. and 199th L.T.M.B. will embus at MONTREAL CAMP (H.19.b.5.8.) at 8.20 a.m. Party from 544 Coy. A.S.C. at X roads (G.29.b. central) at 8.30 a.m.

   A. In addition to the above battalions will detail a party of at least 3 O.R's on bicycles to meet the officer in charge of their advanced billeting party at the AREA COMMANDANT'S Office, BERTHEN at 9 a.m. These men will be available as guides to meet lorries, supply wagons etc.

(-2-)

ADVANCED BILLETING PARTIES.
(Continued).

B. Officer in charge of billeting parties will carefully reconnoitre the best route to guide the personnel and transport of their units from BERTHEN to the Area allotted to them, prior to 11 a.m on the 24th inst.

3. GUIDES.

Guides will meet units at the Cross Roads BERTHEN, (R.22.c.6.8.) at 11 a.m. on the 24th inst.
Guides will also be detailed to meet the supply wagons of the Train Coy. at 12 noon. All guides will be detailed regimentally from the parties mentioned in Para.2.

4. TRANSPORT.

First Line Transport and Train baggage wagons will accompany units on the march. Distances as laid down in 199th Inf. Bde. Order G.46 of 29.9.17. will be adhered to.
The Headquarters of the 544 Coy. A.S.C. and the Train Supply wagons will move in rear of Brigade Group. Guides for Supply Wagons to be at Cross Roads BERTHEN (R.22.c.6.8) at 11 a.m. as detailed above.
                                                                    12 NOON

5. RATIONS.

Rations will be drawn on 23rd inst from Refilling Point by Regimental Transport.
On the 24th inst. rations for consumption on the 25th. will be delivered to units by the Supply Wagons of the Train in the new Area. The 204th and 202nd Machine Gun Coy's will draw their rations on the 24th from refilling point; on the 25th rations will be delivered to them on arrival in new area for consumption on the 26th inst.

6. REAR PARTIES.

Units will each leave a rear party under an officer, for the purpose of cleaning the camp vacated. These parties will follow independently.

7. RAILHEAD.

The Railhead will probably change to EBBLINGHEM on the 25th inst.

8. LORRIES.

Lorries will be allotted as follows for the move on the 24th inst.

Bde. H.Q.	1½ lorries
2/7th Manch.R.	2½ "
2/6th " "	3 "
2/5th " "	3 "
2/8th " "	3 "
199th L.T.M.B.	1 "
	14.

(-3-)

LORRIES.
(Continued).

Ten lorries for the 2/5th, 2/6th, 2/7th Bns. Manch.Regt. and Bde.H.Q. as detailed above will report at Brigade Headquarters BELGIAN CHATEAU at 8 a.m. on the 24th inst.

The 2/5th Manch.Regt. will detail an officer to allot the lorries (in accordance with above instructions) to guides to be sent by units.

Four lorries for 2/6th Manch.Regt. and 199th L.T.M.B. are to report at MONTREAL CAMP (H.19.b.5.8.) at 8.15 a.m. on the 24th inst.

Two lorries for 204th and 202nd Machine Gun Coys. are to report to an officer detailed by 204th Machine Gun Coy. at Cross Roads, CAFE BELGE, (H.29.b.7.5.) at 8 a.m. on the 25th inst.

The ten lorries reporting at BELGIAN CHATEAU on the 24th inst. will proceed to AREA COMMANDANT'S Office at BERTHEN by the following route :-
   Cross Roads CAFE BELGE (H.29.b.7.5.) - DICKEBUSCH - LA CLYTE
   - Cross Roads (M.17.c.6.5.) - WESTOUTRE - and are to be clear
   of Cross Roads CAFE BELGE by 9.30 a.m.

The four lorries reporting at MONTREAL CAMP will also proceed to BERTHEN by shortest routes and be clear of MONTREAL CAMP by 9 a.m. Commanding Officers will arrange for guides from advanced parties to be waiting for lorries at Area Commandant's Office, BERTHEN, - and will also arrange to send an officer with a map with the leading lorry of their group.

9. **LOADING PARTIES.**

Units will detail a loading party of 1 N.C.O. and 4 men to accompany each lorry. These are not to be exceeded (except one officer guide).

10. **TRAIN WAGONS.**

Train wagons for conveyance of baggage will report at the Q.M.Stores of all battalions, L.T.M.B. and Bde.H.Q. on the evening of the 23rd inst.

Units will inform 544 Coy. A.S.C. direct of the exact location of their Q.M.Stores. The wagons will remain with units for the night of the 23/24th

Captain,
Staff Captain,
199th Infantry Brigade.

Distribution :-

Copy No. 1....Brigadier-General.	Copy No. 15...544 Coy.A.S.C.
" " 2....Brigade Major.	" " 16...66th Divl.Train.
" " 3....Staff Captain.	" " 17...66th Division, "G"
" " 4....Bde.Signal Officer.	" " 18...66th " "Q"
" " 5....2/5th Manch.Regt.	" " 19...Area Cmdt.BERTHEN.
" " 6....2/6th "	" " 20...War Diary.
" " 7....2/7th "	" " 21... "
" " 8....2/8th "	" " 22...File.
" " 9....Q.M. 2/5th.Manch.Regt.	" " 23...Spare.
" " 10....Q.M. 2/6th "	" " 24...
" " 11....Q.M. 2/7th "	
" " 12....204th M.G.Coy.	
" " 13....199th L.T.M.B.	
" " 14....202nd M.G.Coy.	

Addendum to 199th Infantry Brigade
ADMINISTRATION ORDER
No. 30.

1. **LORRIES.**

   The 4 lorries for 2/8th Manch. Regt. and 199th L.T.M.B. will report at MONTREAL CAMP at 8 a.m. and will be clear of the camp by 9.30 a.m. on the 24th inst. instead of by 9 a.m.

   The 10 lorries for 2/5th, 2/6th, 2/7th Bns. Manch. Regt. and Bde. H.Q. will be allotted to guides of above battalions by an officer to be detailed from Bde. H.Q. and not from 2/5th Manch. Regt.
   These lorries are to be clear of Cross roads CAFE BEIGE by 10 a.m.

2. **GUIDES.**

   2/8th Manch. Regt. will arrange for guides to meet lorries both at MONTREAL CAMP and at Road Junction K.14.b.6.9. at 7.45 a.m.

3. **BILLETS.**

   Approximate location of billets 2/6th Manch. Regt.

   For K.24.a. & c   read   R.34 a & c.

4. **REAR PARTIES.**

   Rear parties will be left at discretion of Os.C. Units.

                                           Captain,
                                           Staff Captain,
B.H.Q.   199th Infantry Brigade.
23.11.17.

SECRET　　　　　　　　　　　　　　　　　　　　　　　　Copy No. 10

199th Infantry Brigade.
Administrative Order No. 31. (Preliminary Order for move of 199th Brigade Group to CAESTRE Area.

Ref Sheet 27. 1/40.CCC

BILLETS. 1. On the 26th instant the 199th Infantry Brigade Group will move into Billets in the STAPLE No. 2 (Eastern) Area.
The approximate Areas allotted to Units will be as follows:

Unit.	Area.	Headquarters.
Brigade Headquarters.	CAESTRE.	W.3.a.3.6.
2/5th Manchesters.	W.9.13 & 14.	W.19.a.8.3.
2/6th Manchesters.	V.11,12,17 & 23.	V.11.a.3.9.
2/7th Manchesters.	P.30, 36, V.6.	P.30.a.3.3.
2/8th Manchesters.	W.2.8 & 9.	CAESTRE.
204th M.G.Coy	P.35.d.	P.35.a.4.2.
199th L.T.M.B.	P.36. a & c.	P.36.a.8.2.
544 Coy A.S.C.	W.20.c.	W.20.c.1.8.
2/3rd Field Amb.	Q.33.c.	Q.33.c.2.4.

Sketch maps of approximate billeting Areas will be sent to Battalions to-night.

ADVANCE BILLETING PARTIES.
2. Billeting parties will be as set down in Administrative Order No. 30 of 22.11.17 with the addition of 1 Officer and 2 Other Ranks of the 2/3rd Field Ambulance.
These parties will embus to-morrow the 25th inst. as follows :-

Unit.	Embus at.	Time.
B.H.Q.	B.Hqrs. R.32.c.5.8.	8-0 a.m.
2/7th Manchesters.	"	"
2/3rd Field Amb.	"	"
199th L.T.M.B.	"	"
2/6th Manchesters.	"X" Roads, Les 4 Fils Aymon.(X.4.c.3.5.)	8-10 a.m.
544 Coy A.S.C.	"	"
2/5th Manchesters.	Road Junction (X.7.d.75.40).	8-25 a.m.
2/8th Manchesters.	"	"

Unexpended portion of the days rations and rations for the 26th inst will be carried by these parties.
In addition to the above battalions will detail a party of at least 3 O.R's on bicycles to meet the Officer in charge of their advanced billeting party at the Area Commandants Office CAESTRE at 10-0 a.m. These men will be available as guides to meet lorries, supply wagons etc.
Officer in charge of billeting parties will carefully reconnoitre the best route to guide the personnel and Transport of their units from CAESTRE to the Areas allotted to them, prior to 10-0 a.m. on the 26th inst.

GUIDES. 3. Guides will meet units on the 26th inst at the "X" Roads (W.3.a.6.5.) in CAESTRE at an hour to be notified later.
Guides will also be detailed to meet lorries and the supply wagons of the Train. All guides will be detailed Regimentally from the parties mentioned in para.2.

P.T.O.

(-2-)

RATIONS. 4. Rations will be delivered to Units by Supply wagons on 25th for consumption on 26th and on arrival in new Area on 26th for consumption on 27th.

5. ACKNOWLEDGE.

                                                                      Gerald _____
                                                                      Captain.
                                                                   Staff Captain.
                                                          199th Infantry Brigade.

DISTRIBUTION.

```
Copy No. 1........Brigadier-General.
         2........Brigade Major.
         3........Staff Captain.
         4........Bde. Signal Officer.
         5........C.O. 2/5th Manchesters.
         6........  "  2/6th      "
         7........  "  2/7th      "
         8........  "  2/8th      "
         9........  "  204th M.G.Company.
        10........  "  199th L.T.M.Battery.
        11........66th Division "G"
        12........66th Division "Q"
        13........Q.M. 2/5th Manchesters.
        14........  "  2/6th      "
        15........  "  2/7th      "
        16........  "  2/8th      "
        17........544 Coy A.S.C.
        18........2/3rd Field Ambulance.
        19........)
        20........)War Diary
        21........)File.
        22........)
        23........)Spare.
        24........)
        25........202nd M.G.Coy.
```

SECRET.
Copy No...... 10
25.11.17.

199th Infantry Brigade
ADMINISTRATIVE ORDER
No:32.

LORRIES. 1. Lorries will be allotted as follows for move on the 26th inst.

    Bde. H.Q.   1 lorry.
    2/7th Manch.R.   3 lorries.
    2/6th " "   3 "
    2/5th " "   3 "
    2/8th " "   3 "
    199th L.T.M.B.   1 "
    204th M.G.Coy.   1 "
           Total-15 ".

The above mentioned units will detail guides to report to an officer at Brigade Headquarters at BERTHEN, R.32.c.5.8. at 8 a.m. on 26th inst.
Commanding Officers will arrange for guides from advance parties to meet lorries at cross roads W.3.a.6.5. CAESTRE and will also arrange to send officer with a map with leading lorry of their group.
Lorries will be clear of BERTHEN area by 10.30 a.m.

LOADING
PARTIES. 2. Units will detail a loading party of 1 N.C.O. and 4 men to accompany each lorry. These numbers are not to be exceeded (except for one officer guide).

TRANSPORT. 3. First line transport and Train baggage wagons will accompany units in the march. Distances as laid down in 199th Infantry Brigade Order G.46 of 29.9.17. will be adhered to. The Headquarters of the 544 Coy. A.S.C. and the Train supply wagons will move independently and will be clear of FLETRE by 9.30 a.m. Guides for supply wagons to be at cross roads W.3.a.6.5. CAESTRE at 10 a.m. on the 26th.

                        Gerald Unsworth Captain,
                        Staff Captain,
                        199th Infantry Brigade.

Distribution.

Copy No.1...Brigadier-General.	No.14...Q.M.2/6th M.R.
" " 2...Brigade Major.	" 15...Q.M.2/7th "
" " 3...Staff Captain.	" 16...Q.M.2/8th "
" " 4...Bde.Signal Officer.	" 17...544 Coy.A.S.C.
" " 5...C.O.2/5th Manch.Regt.	" 18...2/3rd Fld.Amb.
" " 6... " 2/6th " "	" 19...War Diary.
" " 7... " 2/7th " "	" 20... " "
" " 8... " 2/8th " "	" 21...File.
" " 9... " 204th M.G.Coy.	" 22...Spare.
" " 10... " 199th L.T.M.B.	" 23... "
" " 11...66th Division, "G"	" 24...202nd M.G.Coy.
" " 12...66th " "Q"	
" " 13...Q.M. 2/5th Manch.Regt.	

ADDENDUM TO

199th Infantry Brigade

ADMINISTRATIVE ORDER No: 32.

Officers in charge of Advance Parties have been informed that guides for units are to be at cross roads W.3.a.6.5, CAESTRE at 10.30 a.m. on 26th inst; for lorries at 10 a.m. and supply wagons at 10 a.m.
Train wagons will report to units at 8 a.m. on the 26th inst.

25.11.17.
Gerald Unsworth Captain,
Staff Captain,
199th Infantry Brigade.

SECRET.

Copy No.6

WARNING ORDER No.2.

1. The 199th Infantry Brigade will probably move on the 10th inst. by train.

2. Entrain ESLINGHEM. Detrain GODEWAERDE.

3. Area. - WESTOUTRE.

4. Transport probably move by road.

5. Details follow.

6. Acknowledge.

                                                          Captain,
                                             Brigade Major,
B.H.Q.   199th Infantry Brigade.
8.11.17.

O.C.
   2/5th Bn Manchester Regt.
   2/6th "   "   "
   2/7th "   "   "
   2/8th "   "   "
   204th Machine Gun Coy.
   199th L.T.M.Battery.
   2/3rd Field Ambulance.
   544 Coy. A.S.C.
   199th Signals.

SECRET.   Copy No......

199th Infantry Brigade
ORDER NO. 65.

Ref: sheets 27 & 28. 1/40,000.
HAZEBROUCK 5A.

1. (a) The 66th Division (less Artillery and all Transport) will move by train on the 8th, 9th and 10th Nov. to the WESTOUTRE AREA, and will relieve the 1st Australian Division on the front BROODSEINDE TIBUR. Relief to be complete by Nov. 11th.

    (b) 66th Division will be under the tactical command of 1st ANZAC CORPS until Nov. 15th.

2. (a) The 199th Infantry Brigade Group (less transport) will entrain at EBBLINGHEM and detrain at OUDEZEEM on Nov. 9th.

    (b) Entraining and March Table is attached.

    (c) Orders for move of transport have already been issued by Staff Captain.

3. After the relief in the line is complete the 199th Infantry Brigade Group will be disposed in the CANAL AREA, Brigade H.Q. BELGIAN CHATEAU in H.23. A location list is attached.

4. Code names and station code calls will be taken into use.

5. 2/7th Manch. Regt. will detail one complete company to be permanently attached to the 432nd Field Coy. until further orders. This company will join the 432nd Field Coy. in the WESTOUTRE area on the morning of the 10th. inst.

6. (a) O.C. 432nd Field Coy. will detail an advance party on bicycles to report to Area Commandant, WESTOUTRE as early as possible to obtain details of billets. The officer in charge of this party will report to Lieut. TURPIN, billeting officer of the 199th Infantry Brigade at the Area Commandant's office, WESTOUTRE, who will notify him location of 432nd Field Coy.

    (b) O.C. 432nd Field Coy. will make his own arrangements as regards guides meeting his company.

    (c) 432nd Field Coy. will move by road to WESTOUTRE area from ST. MARIE CAPPEL on Nov. 9th. Time of starting and route at discretion of O.C. Field Company.

7. A list of H.Q. in the CANAL AREA to which the Brigade moves on 10.11.17. is attached.

8. Entrainment states will be prepared and handed to entraining officer (to be detailed by Brigade H.Q.) on the platform.

9. ACKNOWLEDGE.

Captain,
Brigade Major,
199th Infantry Brigade.

B.H.Q.
8.11.17.

P.T.O.

Distribution :-

Copy No. 1....Brigadier-General.
"   "   2....Brigade Major.
"   "   3....Staff Captain.
"   "   4....Brigade Signal Officer.
"   "   5....2/5th. Manch. Regt.
"   "   6....2/6th   "   "
"   "   7....2/7th   "   "
"   "   8....2/8th   "   "
"   "   9....204th Machine Gun Coy.
"   " 10....199th T.M. Battery.
"   " 11....432nd Field Coy. R.E.
"   " 12....2/3rd Field Ambulance.
"   " 13....66th Division, "G"
"   " 14....66th   "   "Q"
"   " 15....C.R.E.
"   " 16....R.T.O. REDLINGHEM.
"   " 17....War Diary
"   " 18.... "   "
"   " 19....File.
"   " 20....Spare.
"   " 25...."

MOVE TABLE.

DATE.	UNIT.	ROUTE.	DESTINATION.	REMARKS.
Nov.9th.	2/5th Manch.R. 204th M.G.Coy. Bde.H.Q. & Signals. 193th T.M.B. 2/6th Manch.R.	By train at 8.22 a.m. from EBBLINGHEM. 9.45	GUDERZOM STATION for WESTOUTRE AREA. Arrive GUDERZOM 10.40 a.m.	The platform at EBBLINGHEM STA. is between the main road and the line at T.24.a.7.2. Troops will be formed up ready to entrain in the order shown in column 2, from west to east, by 7.45 a.m. 2/5th Manch.R. is allotted road from U.7.b.1.2. - EBBLINGHEM. 2/6th Manch.R. will move by main HAZEBROUCK - ARQUES road. 204th Machine Gun Coy. will follow 2/5th Manch.Regt. from billets. No restrictions as regards route of B.H.Q. and L.T.M.B. Commence entraining - 7.45 a.m.
	2/7th Manch.R. 2/7th " " 2/3rd Fld.Art.	By train at 16.22 p.m. from EBBLINGHEM.	"	2/7th Manch.Regt. will approach the station from the east along the main HAZEBROUCK - ARQUES ROAD. 2/7th Manch.R. to clear U.20.a.6.2. by 3.10 p.m. 2/6th Manch.Regt. not to pass this point before 3.15 p.m. 2/7th Manch.R. will entrain at the west end of the platform. 2/3rd Field Ambulance will march via STAPLE - U.7.b.1.2. - EBBLINGHEM. All units to be in position ready at 3.45 p.m. at which hour entrainment commences. N.B. - Guides meet all units at GUDERZOM STATION.
Nov.10th.	199th Inf.Bde. Group (less 2/3rd Field Ambulance).	RENINGHELST - DICKEBUSCH - TUISSINIST.	CANAL AREA.	March to be completed by L.05 p.m. March orders will be issued later. 2/3rd Field Ambulance comes under orders of A.D.M.S. at WESTOUTRE.

SECRET   Copy No 7

199 Inf. Bde. Order No.66

Ref. Sheet 28 / 40,000

1. The 199th Inf. Bde. group will move tomorrow to Belgian CHAU & CANAL AREA in accordance with attached table.

2. Under orders of I Anzac Corps, signal units of 1st Aus Div will remain in present areas until readjustment of the necessary communications has been completed.

3. Detailed instructions for relief of the RE & FD Ambs. are being issued by CRE & ADMS respectively.

4. Careful record will be kept by all units of any defence schemes, maps, area or trench stores, intelligence or battle equipt. handed over.

5. Administrative instructions are being issued separately.

6. (a) After midnight of 10/11 Nov. 16 MGs of 3rd Aus. MG Coy will be relieved on barrage work by 16 guns of 204 MG Coy.

   (b) Exact times of relief and guides will be arranged mutually by O.Cs concerned.

   (c) A guide from 3rd A.M.G Coy will meet 204 MG Coy at MENIN GATE at 3.0 a.m. on the 11th.

   (d) All tripods & belt boxes will be handed over by 3rd A.M.G. Coy. Tripods & boxes to replace will be drawn at Transport lines of

(2)

204 M.G. Coy under Coy arrangements.
(e) Location of 3rd A.M.G Coy is D.27.a.1.5.

7. The following are the arrangements as regards working parties.

(a). 1 Coy 2/7 Man Reg. for attachment to 432nd F.D. Coy R.E. will move at 8.0 a.m. to join 432nd F.D Coy at DARBY CAMP G 32 d.3.3.

(b). 2 Coys. 2/7 Man Reg to relieve 2 Coys 7th A.1. Bn. must be made up to working strength of 200 each by the addition of a complete unit, section or platoon as required. They will take over from 2 Coys 7th A.1.Bn. in the GORDON AREA (E.of YPRES) before 6.0 p.m. Guides will be provided by 7th A.1.Bn. from camp at H.18.c.3.7. Cookers and transport will be taken if possible.

(c). 1 Bn. for Ry. work (2/6 M.R). Work appears to require usually 60 men for night, 200 men by day (7.30 a.m - 4.0 p.m.). The Bn. receives orders direct from the R.E. under whom they are working, then return to camp after work. Work orders are forwarded daily.

8. Bde H.Q. will close at WESTOUTRE at 9.0 a.m. and reopen at CHAU. BELGE at 10.30 a.m.

9. ACKNOWLEDGE.

R. L. Bond
Capt.

9.11.17

Copy no. 7. 199 L.T.M.B. Bde Maj. 199 Inf Bde.

MARCH TABLE to accompany 199 Inf. Bde. Order No. 66

Units	Starting Pt	Time	Route	Destination	Remarks
2/7 M.R.	R⁰ pnt. g.35.c.o.6.	8.18 a.m.	RENINGHELST – ZEVECOTEN – Rd jnc. G.30.c.50.99 – HALLEBAST – DICKEBUSH – Rd jnc. H.18.c.9.	Camp H.18.c.3.7.	—
2/6 M.R.		8.36 a.m.		" H.18.c.3.4.	—
2/5 M.R.		9.04 "		" H.24.a.0.8.	—
199 L.T.M.B.		9.22 "		" H.24.a.3.9.	Last 3 huts in 2/5 M.R. lines.
204 M.G.Coy.		9.27 "		Chau SEGARD. H.30.	
B.H.Q.		9.37 "		H.23.b.3.7.	
2/8 M.R.	—	—	—	—	Remains in WESTOUTRE AREA till Nov. 12, when it moves to DOMINION LINES (9.23.b) until
544 (Coy) A.S.C.	—	—	—	g.22.d.4.3.	moves independently. Clears camps between 9.30 & 10.0 a.m.
432 F.P. Coy	—	—	—	H.24.a.7.7.	moves under orders of C.R.E.

SECRET.   Copy No. 10.

199th Infantry Brigade.
WARNING ORDER.

1. (a) On the night of the 19th/20th the 198th Infantry Brigade is relieving the 197th Infantry Brigade in the line.

    (b) The 197th Infantry Brigade on relief is going into 198th Infantry Brigade billets in YPRES.

    (c) After 10.0 a.m. on the 20th Nov. the 199th Infantry Brigade will take over billets occupied by 197th Infantry Brigade in YPRES. No troops of 197th Infantry Bde. to leave their quarters until actually relieved by corresponding units of 199th Infantry Brigade.

2. Machine Guns will be relieved at times other than during the night 19/20th. Nov.

3. The following working parties will be taken over by 197th Infantry Brigade.

    (a) One Battalion (2/6th Manch.Regt.) working on railways under 9th Canadian Railway Troops Coy.

    (b) Two companies of 2/7th Manchester Regt. on roads etc. billeted in GORTON AREA under 146th. Army Troops Coy. Coy. R.E.
    Other working parties and details will not be relieved.

4. Detailed orders for relief will be issued later.

5. ACKNOWLEDGE.

                                            R. L. Banks
                                            Captain,
                                            Brigade Major,
16.11.17.   199th Infantry Brigade.

Distribution :-

Copy No. 1.....Brigadier-General.   Copy No. 8.....2/8th Manch.Regt.
  "   "   2.....Brigade Major.   "   "   9.....204th M.G.Coy.
  "   "   3.....Staff Captain.   "   "   10.....199th L.T.M.B.
  "   "   4.....Bde. Signal Officer.   "   "   11.....544 Coy.A.S.C.
  "   "   5.....2/5th Manch.Regt.   "   "   12.....War Diary.
  "   "   6.....2/6th   "   "   "   "   13.....   "   "
  "   "   7.....2/7th   "   "   "   "   14.....File.
                                           "   "   15.....Spare.
                                           "   "   16..... "

SECRET.   Copy No...10.

199th Infantry Brigade
ORDER NO: 67.

Ref: Sheet 28, N.W.4. 1/10,000.

1. (a) On 19th Nov, and the night of the 19/20th Nov, the 198th Inf. Bde. is relieving 197th Inf. Bde. in the line. On relief the 197th Inf. Bde. moves into billets vacated by 198th Inf. Bde.

   (b) On Nov. 20th, after 10.0 a.m. the 199th Inf. Bde. with exception of 2/8th Manchesters, will take over billets in YPRES area from 197th Inf. Bde. which takes over billets from 199th Inf. Bde. in CANAL AREA.

2. A relief table is attached.

3. The following working parties will be taken over by 197th Inf. Bde, AFTER completion of day work on Nov.20th.

   (a) Railway work carried out under 9th Canadian Railway Troops Coy. by 2/6th Manch.Regt. will be taken over by 3/5th Lanc.Fuslrs.

   (b) The companies of the 2/7th Manch.Regt. accommodated in GORDON AREA and CAVALRY BARRACKS will be relieved on work under 145th Army Troops Company, R.E. by 2 companies of 2/6th Lanc.Fslrs. who will take over above billets.

4. The following working parties will <u>not</u> be taken over
   (a) 100 men 2/5th Manch.Regt. working under Canadian Tunnelling Co.
   (b) Parties and fatigues detailed under instructions issued by "Q" branch 66th Division.

5. 2/8th Manch.Regt. will relieve 2/4th East Lancashire Regt. and take over the working parties found by them, on Nov.19th. 2 Coys. 2/4th E.Lancs. are accommodated in RAILWAY Dugouts, 1.Company in GORDON AREA and H.Q. and 1 Company in Infantry Barracks YPRES. Details of relief to be arranged between O.s. C. concerned.

6. Billetting arrangements will be made as follows. Billeting parties will be sent to new billets before the corresponding units of 198th Inf. Bde. have left, and will remain there during the period of occupation by 197th Inf. Bde.
   O.C.s. and Company Commanders will get into touch with their opposite numbers of 198th Inf. Bde. as soon as possible.

7. ACKNOWLEDGE.

                                                    R.L.Brand
                                                    Captain,
                                                    Brigade Major,
                                                    199th Infantry Brigade.

B.H.Q.
17.11.17.
                                                    P.T.O.

Distribution :-

Copy No. 1.....Brigadier-General.
"   "   2.....Brigade Major.
"   "   3.....Staff Captain.
"   "   4.....Bde. Signal Officer.
"   "   5.....2/5th Manch. Regt.
"   "   6.....2/6th   "   "
"   "   7.....2/7th   "   "
"   "   8.....2/8th   "   "
"   "   9.....204th M.G.Coy.
"   " 10.....199th L.T.M.B.
"   " 11.....544 Coy. A.S.C.
"   " 12.....197th Inf. Bde.
"   " 13..... "   "   "
"   " 14.....198th   "   "
"   " 15.....66th Division, "G"
"   " 16.....66th   "   "Q"
"   " 17.....Area Commandant, CANAL AREA.
"   " 18.....War Diary.
"   " 19..... "   "
"   " 20.....File.
"   " 21.....Spare.
"   " 22..... "

RELIEF TABLE.

Date.	Unit.	From.	To.	Time of reaching new area.	Billets in YPRES occupied on 18/19th Nov.	Billets in YPRES occupied on 19/20th.	REMARKS.
19th.	2/8th Manch.R.	MONTREAL LINES	INFANTRY BARRACKS (Bn.HQ.)etc.				See para. 5.
20th.	Bde. H.Q.	CHAU. BELGE	"		2/4th E.Lancs.		
"	2/5th Manch.R.	CANAL AREA	Esplanade Sap.	10.15 am.	198th Inf.Bde.	2/8th L.F.s.	
"	2/6th "	"	Canal Dugouts.	11.00 am.	2/5th Manc.L.R.		
					2/10th M.R.	3/5th L.F.s	Working parties rejoin Battalions in YPRES area at work.
"	2/7th "	"	INFANTRY BARRACKS.	11.45 am.	2/5th E.Lancs.	2/6th L.F.s.	"
"	199th L.T.M.B.	"	Esplanade Sap.	12.30 pm.	198th L.T.M.B.	199th LTMB.	"
"	204th M.G.Coy.						Stands fast.

SECRET   Copy No. 9

199th Infantry Brigade Order No. 68

Ref; Sheets 27 & 28
1/40.000

1. The 199th Infantry Brigade (less 204th M.G.Coy) will move from YPRES to CANAL Area to-morrow, November 22nd, taking over Billets vacated by 197th Infantry Brigade.

2. March Table for above move is attached.

3. (a) On November 24th 199th Infantry Brigade Group (less 204th M.G.Coy and Field Coy. R.E) moves to BERTHEN Area via RENINGHELST.
   (b) On November 25th 202nd and 204th M.G.Companies move from Chateau SEGARD Area to BERTHEN via RENINGHELST.
   (c) On November 26th, 199th Infantry Brigade Group (less Field Coy. R.E.) and 202nd M.G.Coy. move to STAPLE Area, Sub-Area No. 2 (Eastern).
   (d) Detailed Orders for (a), (b), (c) will be issued later.

4. (a) One Coy 2/7th Manchester Regiment affiliated to 432nd Field Company R.E. will rejoin its Battalion in CANAL Area on Nov. 23rd.
   (b) Party of 100 Other Ranks attached to 1st Canadian Tunnelling Coy. at LA CLYTTE will rejoin 2/5th Manchester Regiment in CANAL Area on November 23rd at noon.
   (c) Party of 10 Other Ranks engaged on carrying wireless: Instructions for relief will be issued later.

5. 2/3rd Field Ambulance from WIPPENHOEK will rejoin 199th Infantry Brigade Group on the march from BERTHEN Area on November 26th. Orders for this move will be issued later.

6. Brigade Headquarters will close at Infantry Barracks YPRES at 12.15 p.m. and re-open at CHAU BELGE at the same hour on November 22nd.

7. ACKNOWLEDGE.

                                                    Captain.
                                                    Brigade Major.
                                                    199th Infantry Brigade.

DISTRIBUTION.

Copy No. 1....Brigadier-General.
        2....Brigade Major.
        3....Staff Captain.
        4....2/5th Manchesters.
        5....2/6th   "
        6....2/7th   "
        7....2/8th   "
        8....204th M.G.Coy.
        9....199th L.T.M. Battery.
       10....197th Inf. Brigade.
       11....198th   "
       12....C.R.E.
       13....A.D.M.S.
       14....544 Coy A.S.C.
       15....202nd M.G.Coy.
       16....2/3rd Fld Ambulance.
       17..).War Diary
       18..)
       19, 20, 21...(Spare.
       22...66th Division "G"
       23...66th Division "Q"

March Table to accompany 199th Infantry Brigade Order No. 68

Date.	Unit.	From.	To.	TIME. Head of Unit passes BELGIAN BATTERY CORNER.	REMARKS.
Nov. 22nd.	2/8th Man;R.	INF. BARRACKS YPRES	MONTREAL CAMP	10-0 a.m.	
"	2/6th Man.R.	KRUISSTRAAT	CANAL AREA	10-30 a.m.	
"	2/5th Man;R.	ESPLANADE SAP.	"	11-0 a.m.	
"	2/7th Man;R.	INFANTRY BKS.	"	11-30 a.m.	
"	199th L.T.M.B.	ESPLANADE SAP.	"	12-0 noon.	
"	Bde. H.Q.	INF.BARRACK.	CIAU. BELGE.	12-15 p.m.	
"	200 M.G.Coy.	Stands Fast.			Relieves Guns in Line under instructions contained in 464/26/G of 20.11.17.

N.B. Billetting parties will report to Area Commandants of new Areas the previous day to that on which the Brigade moves into the new area, under arrangements to be made by Staff Captain.

B Casualty   Copy   Army Form W.3210.

Serial No. 25   Service in France

Corps:- 199 Bde L.T.M.B.

No. 303341. Rank. Pte. Name. Bryant W

Age   Service   Religion.

Disease or Wound:- G.W. Hand & r. Shoulder

                              A.T.S. 500

Serial Number

10
C.C.S.

SECRET.   Copy No. 10

                                                                       22.11.17.

                        199th INFANTRY Brigade

                              ORDER No.69.
                              _____

                        Ref: Sheets 27 & 28.

1. The 199th Infantry Brigade Group (less 204th Machine Gun Coy. and
   432nd Field Coy. R.E and 2/3rd Field Ambulance) will move from
   CANAL AREA to BERTHEN Area on November 24th.

2. March table is attached.

3. Guides under arrangements made by Staff Captain will be ready to meet
   units in BERTHEN at 11 a.m.

4. Advance parties proceeding to BERTHEN on Nov.23rd. will arrange to
   reconnoitre carefully best routes for men and for transport to
   billeting areas from BERTHEN.

5. (a) 202nd Machine Gun Coy. and 204th Machine Gun Coy. will move
       from CHAU.SEGARD area to BERTHEN area on Nov.25th.

   (b) These two companies will march under orders of O.C. 202nd
       Machine Gun Coy. No restrictions as to time. Route as laid
       down in attached march table for remainder of the Brigade Group.

6. Brigade Headquarters will close at CHATEAU BELGE at 8.30 a.m. and
   reopen at BERTHEN on arrival.

7. ACKNOWLEDGE.

                                                    Captain,
                                               Brigade Major,
                                          199th Infantry Brigade.

Distribution :-

    Copy No.1.....Brigadier-General.   Copy No.11...544 Coy.A.S.C.
     "   " 2.....Brigade Major.   "   " 12...202nd M.G.Coy.
     "   " 3.....Staff Captain.   "   " 13..66th Division,"G"
     "   " 4.....Bde.Signal Officer.   "   " 14...66th   "   "G"
     "   " 5.....2/5th Manch.Regt.   "   " 15...War Diary.
     "   " 6.....2/6th   "   "   "   " 16... "   "
     "   " 7.....2/7th   "   "   "   " 17..File.
     "   " 8.....2/8th   "   "   "   " 18...Spare.
     "   " 9.....204th Machine Gun Coy.   "   " 19... "
     "   " 10.....199th L.T.M.B.

MARCH TABLE TO ACCOMPANY

199th Infantry Brigade Order No.69.

Date.	Units in order of march.	Starting Point.	Time of passing Starting Point.	Destination. (Sheet 27I.)	Route.	Remarks.
Nov.24th	2/8th Manch.R.	X Roads H.19.B.4.9. Regiment H.15.d.9.2.	8.10 a.m.	X.1.a.	H.16.d.3.3. - H.13.d.9.2. - ZEVECOTEN - MENINGHIST - WESTOUTRE (M.9.c.55.50) - M.8.c.1.3 - X roads H.16.c. - BERTHEN.	
"	199th L.T.M.B.	"	8.28 a.m.	R.21.a.		
"	2/5th Manch.R.	X roads H.16.d.2.2.	8.0 a.m.	R.32 & 33.		
"	2/6th	"	8.18 a.m.	R.33 & 34.		
"	2/7th	"	8.36 a.m.	R.27 & 28.		
"	Bde.H.Q.	"	9.04 a.m.	BERTHEN.		
"	544 Coy.A.S.C.	X roads G.34.d.3.0.	10.34 a.m.	FILS AYMON X.4.c.		
25th	202nd M.G.Coy.		—	) X.2 & 0.		
"	204th M.G.Coy.		—	)		

O.C. 204 MG Coy
  " 199 LTMB
[" 2/7 Man Reg for information]

1. Ref. march table for tomorrow, 2/7 Man
(sent by despatch) Reg. are proceeding by route as follows
BERTHEN — R.20.B.4.7 — R.14.d.3.2 —
R.20.a.1.8 — R.19.b.2.8 — R.19.a.5.2
— R.19.d.6.5 — R.25.B.2.8 — THIEUSHOUST
— CAESTRE.

2. 199 LTMB will march in rear of
2/7 Man Reg. and will be prepared to move
about 10.30 a.m.

3. 204 MG Coy will move by the above
route, starting not before 1.0 p.m.

25.11.17   R H Bond
                              Capt
                          Bde Maj. 199 Inf Bde.

SECRET.   Copy No. 10
                                                           25.11.17.

                        199th Infantry Brigade
                            ORDER No: 70.
                            ─────────────

                    Ref: Sheet 27 (Belgium & France).

1. The 199th Infantry Brigade Group will move from the BERTHEN Area
   on November 26th. to STAPLE Sub-area No.2. (Eastern).

2. March Table is attached.

3. Guides under arrangements made by Staff Captain will be ready
   to meet units at CAESTRE - Road junction W.6.a.65.

4. Brigade Headquarters will close at BERTHEN at 11.0 a.m. and
   reopen at CAESTRE at the same hour.

5. ACKNOWLEDGE.

                                                    R. L. Bond
                                                        Captain,
                                                    Brigade Major,
                                                199th Infantry Brigade.

Distribution :-

Copy No. 1 ... Brigadier-General.
  "   " 2 ... Brigade Major.
  "   " 3 ... Staff Captain.
  "   " 4 ... Bde. Signal Officer.
  "   " 5 ... 2/5th Manch. Regt.
  "   " 6 ... 2/6th   "   "
  "   " 7 ... 2/7th   "   "
  "   " 8 ... 2/8th   "   "
  "   " 9 ... 204th Machine Gun Coy.
  "   " 10 ... 199th L.T.M. Battery.
  "   " 11 ... 544 Coy. A.S.C.
  "   " 12 ... 2/3rd Field Ambulance.
  "   " 13 ... 432nd Fld. Coy. (O. i/c Transport)
  "   " 14 ... 202nd Machine Gun Coy.
  "   " 15 ... 66th Division, "G"
  "   " 16 ... 66th   "   "Q"
  "   " 17 ... War Diary.
  "   " 18 ...   "   "
  "   " 19 ... 197th Inf. Bde.
  "   " 20 ... File.
  "   " 21 ... Spare.
  "   " 22 ...   "

MARCH TABLE TO ACCOMPANY
199th Infantry Brigade Order No.76.

Date.	Units in order of march.	Starting Point.	Time of passing Starting Point.	Destination. (Sheet No.27)	Route.	Remarks.
Nov 26.	2/5th March.R.	FLETRE X rds. X.1.a.6.9.	10 a.m. 10.15 am	Area IV.W.9,13,14,15.		S/17 March independently via LE ROSSIGNOL - Rd. junction R.25.A.2.8. - THIEUSHOEK - CAESTRE. Not to enter CAESTRE before 12.30 pm
" "	2/6th " "	FLETRE X rds X.1.a.6.9.	10.18 a.m. 10.33 am	" (3) V11,12,17 & 23.		Route to J.P. via METEREN
" "	2/7th " "	FLETRE W.6.c.7.1	11.00	" (2) P30,36,V5 & 6.	Cross Rds X.1.a.00.10. FLETRE - CAESTRE.	
" "	2/8th " "	X rds. X.1.a.8.9	11.4 a.m. 11.19	" (1) W2,3,7,8 & 9.		
" "	Bde.H.Q.	"	11.22 a.m. 11.37	CAESTRE.		
" "	199th L.T.M.B.	"	11.25 a.m. 11.40	P36.a & c.		
" "	2/3rd Fld.Amb.	"		Q.33.c.	March independently via GODEWAERSVELDE & KEMMELHOF. Head of Column not to Cross the roads junction Q.28.c.c.w. before 12.30 p.m.	
" "	204th M.G.Coy.	"		P.35.c.	March independently via FLETRE - not to start before 1 p.m.	
" "	202nd M.G.Coy.	"		STAPLE (West area).	March independently. To be clear of FLETRE by 10 a.m.	
" "	544 Coy.A.S.C.	"		W.20.c.	March independently. To be clear of FLETRE by 9.30 a.m.	
" "				MORBECQUE.		

II

Summary of
Events
for the month

WAR DIARY
INTELLIGENCE SUMMARY.

Summary of Events.

Summary of November.

During the month of November we did not actually go out to our line. We were in Reserve and Support to Brigades of our Division during the period 1/11/17 – 21/11/17 in the CANAL AREA and ESPLANADE SAP YPRES. We were in close during the time bivouac of the hutments. During these periods 4 experimented with methods of dealing with the STOKES MORTAR using smoke bombs which gave us clouds of smoke bombs which these E.A. My other MORTAR fire. During the period 22/11/17 – 30/11/17 a slightly better state of events [xxxx] being in the YPRES AREA. [xxxx between] down (trench fever or slight causes) from the condition of —

30/11/17

[signature] D. Mackinlay Capt.
[signature] O.C. 198th T.M.B.

III

CASUALTY

RETURNS

Army Form W.3091.

Cover for Documents.

Nature of Enclosures.

CONFIDENTIAL   ORIGINAL

WAR DIARY

OF

199th L.T.M. BATTERY.

FROM

1st Dec. — 31st Dec.

~~Notes, or Letters written.~~

VOLUME V

APPENDIX

I. Operation Orders

II. Short Summary of events for the month

Army Form C. 2118.

WAR DIARY
or
INTELLIGENCE SUMMARY.

(Erase heading not required.)

Instructions regarding War Diaries and Intelligence Summaries are contained in F. S. Regs., Part II. and the Staff Manual respectively. Title pages will be prepared in manuscript.

Place	Date	Hour	Summary of Events and Information	Remarks and references to Appendices
ST. SYLVESTRE CAPPEL (CAESTRE AREA)	1917 Dec 1st		Weather Dull. Training. SLG	
"	Dec 2nd		Weather Dull. The Battery changed their billets but remained in the same area. SLG	
"	Dec 3rd		Weather fine Training SLG	
"	Dec 4th		Weather fine Training SLG	
"	Dec 5th		Weather fine Training SLG	
"	Dec 6th		Weather fine Training SLG	
"	Dec 7th		Weather fine Training. Casualties 20 A/5 (sick) SLG	
"	8th		Weather fine Training SLG	
"	9th		Weather fine. Church Parade. SLG	

WAR DIARY or INTELLIGENCE SUMMARY

Army Form C. 2118.

Place	Date	Hour	Summary of Events and Information	Remarks and references to Appendices
ST SYLVESTRE CAPPEL (CAESTRE AREA)	Dec 10		Weather fine. Training. S/by	
	Dec 11		Weather fine. Training. S/by	
	Dec 12		Weather dull. Training. S/by	
	Dec 13		Weather dull. Training. S/by	
	Dec 14		Weather wet. Training. Received Brig. letter G.615. Demand Orders S/by	G.615
	Dec 15		Weather wet. Training. Received Brig. Order No. 1 Copy No. 10. Administrative Order No. 3 Copy No. 10. S/by	Army Order 1 Copy 10 A.O No 1 30 mm O.O No 3
	Dec 16		Weather fine. Church Parade. S/by	
	Dec 17		Weather fine. Training. S/by	
	Dec 18		Weather fine. Training. S/by	
	Dec 19		Weather fine. Holiday for Xmas celebration. S/by	

Army Form C. 2118.

WAR DIARY
or
INTELLIGENCE SUMMARY.
(Erase heading not required.)

Instructions regarding War Diaries and Intelligence Summaries are contained in F. S. Regs., Part II. and the Staff Manual respectively. Title pages will be prepared in manuscript.

Place	Date	Hour	Summary of Events and Information	Remarks and references to Appendices
ST SYLVESTRE CAPPEL (CAETRE AREA)	Dec 20		Weather dull. Training 2Coy	
"	Dec 21		Weather unsettled. Training 2Coy	
"	Dec 22		Weather dull. Training 2Coy	
"	Dec 23		Weather dull. Church parade 2Coy	
"	Dec 24		Weather wet (slush). Training. Subj: firing 2Coy	
"	Dec 25		Snow. Training 2Coy	
"	Dec 26		Snow. Training 2Coy	
"	Dec 27		Weather fine. Subj: firing 2Coy	
"	Dec 28		Weather fine. Training 2Coy	
"	Dec 29		Weather dull. Training 2Coy	
"	Dec 30		Snow. Church parade 2Coy	
"	Dec 31		Weather fine. Training 2Coy Signed [illegible] O/Brig: Comm. Order No. 33 Copy Rec'd	

Operation Orders

O.C.
2/5th Manch.R.
2/6th   "   "
2/7th   "   "
2/8th   "   "
204th M.G.Coy,
199th L.T.M.B.

WARNING ORDER
199th Infantry Brigade.

1. The 199th Infantry Brigade (less 204th Machine Gun Coy. and 199th L.T.M.B.) will move to RENINGHELST and HALIFAX Camp area on Sunday Dec.16th.

2. Brigade moves by bus.

3. Transport moves same day by road.

4. 204th Machine Gun Coy. and 199th L.T.M.B. remain in present billets till further orders.

5. All maps Sheet 27 S.E. issued to battalions will be returned forthwith, corrected to date and showing sites of Rifle Ranges, Assault Courses, bombing pits.

6. Certificates of occupation of ground must be filled in, and *handed back to owner for transmission through the Maire to Rents officer.*

7. Further orders for move will be issued later.

Captain,
Brigade Major,
199th Infantry Brigade.

B.H.Q.
14/12/17.

SECRET.

O.C.,
2/5th Bn Manchester Regt.
2/6th " " " "
2/7th " " " "
2/8th " " " "
200th Machine Gun Coy.
199th L.T.M.Battery.

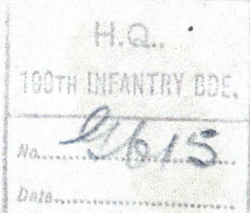
H.Q.
199TH INFANTRY BDE.
No. G615
Date............

1. The 199th Infantry Brigade will move in a few days to a Corps Back Area.

2. The Brigade will be employed under C.E. II ANZAC Corps on work on Corps Line.

3. The 3 Field Companies R.E. are moving by Dec. 15th.

4. Accommodation and daily transport for working parties is being arranged.

R M Bond
Captain,
Brigade Major,
199th Infantry Brigade.

B.H.Q.
14/12/17.

SECRET. 199th Infantry Brigade Copy No. 10

ADMINISTRATIVE ORDER No. 32.

Ref:- Sheet 28.

MOVE. The 199th Infantry Brigade (less 204th M.G.Coy, 199th L.T.M.B. and 2/3rd Field Ambulance) will move to billets as under :-

Bde.H.Q.	RENINGHELST.
2/5th M.R.	DEVONSHIRE CAMP G.22.b.8.6.
2/6th M.R. }	" " " " and Camp at G.22.b.3.3.
2/7th M.R.	WINNIPEG CAMP H.19.b.2.5.
2/8th M.R.	MONTREAL CAMP H.19.b.5.7.
544 Coy.A.S.C.	H.Q. RENINGHELST G.34.b.2.3.

BILLETING PARTIES. Billeting parties of not more than 5 per Unit will report at Brigade Headquarters at 7 a.m. on 18th inst.

TRANSPORT. Lorries will be at the Brigade H.Q. CAESTRE at 7 a.m. and will be allotted as follows:-

Bde.H.Q.	2.
2/7th M.R.	2.
2/8th M.R.	3.

Guides will report at above time and place. One lorry for 2/7th Manch.R. will make two journeys.
The 7 lorries will return to Brigade H.Q. CAESTRE at 12.30 p.m.
3 lorries are allotted to the 2/5th Manch.R. and 3 to the 2/6th Manch.R. Guides from these units report at above time and place.

BAGGAGE WAGONS. Horses for baggage wagons will be sent to Transport lines of units at 7 a.m. by 544 Coy.A.S.C. These wagons will move with 1st line transport.

SUPPLIES - for B.H.Q. 4 Battns. and 544 Coy.A.S.C.

(a) Rations for consumption on the 16th. will be carried by Units. Rations for consumption on the 17th inst. will be carried on supply wagons and delivered to Q.M.Stores. Rations for consumption on the 18th inst. will be drawn from the dump at RENINGHELST, G.35.c.8.4. Time of drawing to be notified later.

(b) For 204th M.G.Coy, 199th L.T.M.B. and 2/3rd Field Amb. on 16th inst, these units will refil as at present at BORRE on and after 17th inst, from the 198th Infantry Brigade group refilling point at ST.MARIE CAPPEL. 204th M.G.Coy. will draw for L.T.M.B.

ORDNANCE. On and after the 17th inst. Units mentioned in (a) above will draw Ordnance stores from dump of 541 Coy.A.S.C. Div.Train. D.A.D.O.S. will communicate time and place of issue direct to units concerned.

AREA STORES. (On charge of units moving)

All area stores will be handed into the Area Commandant, CAESTRE and receipts obtained. Copies of these receipts will be forwarded to Brigade Headquarters by 9 a.m. on 17th inst.

P.T.O.

(2).

GUIDES. Units will arrange for guides to meet their battalions and transport at their debussing point.
Guides will meet supply wagons at 1 p.m. at OUDERDOM fork roads at G.30.A.2.7.

PERSONNEL REMAINING. Two O.Rs. will remain at the Baths, CAESTRE and will be rationed by the 2/3rd Field Ambulance from the 17th inst. Two N.C.O.s. M.M.P. and two horses will be rationed by the 204th M.G.Coy. from the 17th inclusive.

ACKNOELEDGE.

J B Fox Captain,
Staff Captain,
199th Infantry Brigade.

B.H.Q.
15/12/17.

Distribution:-

Copy No. 1.....G.O.C.
"   "   2.....Brigade Major,
"   "   3.....Staff Captain,
"   "   4.....Bde.Signal Officer.
"   "   5.....2/5th Manch.R.
"   "   6.....2/6th   "   "
"   "   7.....2/7th   "   "
"   "   8.....2/8th   "   "
"   "   9.....204th M.G.Coy.
"   "   10.....199th L.T.M.B.
"   "   11.....544 Coy,A.S.C.
"   "   12.....2/3rd Fld.Amb.
"   "   13.....Q.M.2/5th Manch.R.
"   "   14.....Q.M.2/6th   "   "
"   "   15.....Q.M.2/7th   "   "
"   "   16.....Q.M.2/8th   "   "
"   "   17.....66th Division, "G"
"   "   18.....66th   "   "A"
"   "   19.....O.C. 66th Divl.Train.
"   "   20.....Area Commandant, CAESTRE.
"   "   21.....   "   "   RENINGHELST.
"   "   22.....   "   "   HALIFAX Camp.
"   "   23.....War Diary.
"   "   24.....   "   "
"   "   25.....File.
"   "   26.....Spare.
"   "   27..... "

SECRET 199th Infantry Brigade No.......

ORDER No: 71.

Ref: Sheets 27 and 28, 1/40,000.

1. The 199th Infantry Brigade (less 204th M.G.Coy. and 199th L.T.M.B.) will move to the RENINGHELST - HALIFAX CAMP area on Dec.16th.1917, by lorry.

2. 1Transport will move by road.

3. Movement table is attached.

4. (a) The Brigade will be employed on work under the C.E. II ANZAC Corps. Work will commence on Dec.18th.

(b) Battalions will forward *immediately* a statement of total numbers of other ranks (exclusive of necessary proportion of officers and N.C.O.s. for supervisory duties) available for work. Signallers undergoing instruction in the Brigade Class will not be included in these numbers.

5. Two platoons 2/7th Manch.Regt. at present working in YPRES will rejoin their unit on Dec.17th.

6. 204th M.G.Coy, 199th L.T.M.B. and 2/3rd Field Ambulance will remain in present billets.

7. Before leaving the area units should arrange to collect and store as near the work as possible all loose wood, corrugated iron and other material which might be moved by inhabitants during the time the area is unoccupied. Sacks on assault courses should also be dismounted and stored, without being emptied, if convenient storage can be found.

8. Administrative instructions are being issued separately.

9. Brigade Headquarters will close at CAESTRE at 8.0 a.m. and reopen at RENINGHELST on arrival.

10. 544 Coy.A.S.C. moves independently to RENINGHELST. H.Q. G.34.b.2.3.

11. ACKNOWLEDGE.

           R.L.Bond
           Captain,
           Brigade Major,
15/12/17.   199th Infantry Brigade.

Distribution:-

No.1.....	G.O.C.	No.11....	544 Coy.A.S.C.
" 2.....	Brigade Major.	" 12....	2/3rd Fld.Amb.
" 3.....	Staff Captain.	" 13....	66th Division,"G"
" 4.....	Bde.Signal Officer.	" 14....	66th " "A"
" 5.....	2/5th Manch.R.	" 15....	C.R.E.
" 6.....	2/6th " "	" 16....	War Diary.
" 7.....	2/7th " "	" 17....	" "
" 8.....	2/8th " "	" 18....	File.
" 9.....	204th M.G.Coy.	" 19....	Spare.
" 10.....	199th L.T.M.B.	" 20....	"

MOVEMENT TABLE to accompany 1/9th Inf. Bde. Order No.71.

Unit.	Embussing Point. Head of Column.	Time. Ready to embus.	Column moves.	Destination. Debus.	Destination. Camp.	REMARKS.
Bde.H.Q.	W.5.a.5.5.	7.45 a.m.	8.15 a.m.	H.19.b.5.6.	REMINGHELST	As units are embussing separately, C.Os. will have their own arrangements for markers etc, and will be responsible that their respective columns are ready to move off at the times stated in column 4. In each case the head of the column will be at that end of nearest ST. SYLVESTRE CAPPEL through which place all columns move.
2/8th Lanc.R.	W.3.a.5.5.	7.45 a.m.	8.15 a.m.	H.19.b.5.6.	MONTREAL H.19.b.5.6.	
2/7th " "	O.31.a.3.0.	7.30 a.m.	8.0 a.m.	H.19.b.5.6.	WINNIPEG	
2/6th " "	V.16.b.3.2.	12.30 p.m.	1.0 p.m.	G.22.b.5.4.	DEVONSHIRE. G.22.b.8.6.	
2/5th " "	W.19.c.2.3.	12.30 p.m.	1.0 p.m.	"	"	

MOVE OF TRANSPORT.

All transport moves independently, starting from respective transport lines as follows:- 2/8th Lanch.R. 8.30a.m.
                                                                                                    2/7th " " "
                                                                                                      2/6th " " 9.0 a.m.
                                                                                                      2/5th " " "

Guides will meet transport at units debussing points as shown above. No restrictions as regards route.

SECRET.   Copy No. 10

199th Infantry Brigade
ADMINISTRATIVE ORDER No.33.

Ref: Sheet 27.

MOVE.	The 199th Inf.Bde. (less Hove 204th M.G.Coy. 199th L.T.M.B. & 2/3rd Fld. Amb.) will be located in the CAESTRE area in the billets recently occupied by them.
BILLETING PARTIES.	Billeting parties will proceed from Units on day previous to Battalion leaving.
TRANSPORT.	Transport will move independently as shown in table "A"
BAGGAGE & SUPPLY WAGONS.	Baggage and Supply Wagons will report to Units on the day previous to move of Transport.
LORRIES.	Lorries for conveyance of kit will be allotted as shown in attached table "C"
SUPPLIES.	Supply arrangements for all Units moving are shown in attached table "B"
ORDNANCE.	On and after Jan.1st. Ordnance refilling point for 199th Brigade Group will be at HONDEGHEM. Exact location will be notified later.
AREA STORES.	All billet and Area Stores now held by Battalions will be handed over to 197th Brigade and receipts taken.
MEDICAL ARRANGEMENTS.	The sick will on and after the 1st January, be dealt with by the 2/2nd East Lancs. Field Amb. at CAESTRE.
HANDING OVER CAMP TO 197th INF. BDE.	The Battalions of 197th Infantry Brigade will probably arrive at camps 1 hour before the Battalions of 199th Inf.Bde. 'bus. Units will have half their lines cleared by 3 p.m. on the afternoon of relief, ready for the incoming units to occupy. The camps will be handed over as far as possible with

      1. Fires burning in all officers huts.
                  Officers Messes.
                  Sergeants Messes.
                  Q.M.Stores.
                  Cook-houses.

      2. A small supply of fuel for above.

CAMP IMPROVEMENTS.	A list of work in progress to be handed over and a list of all material drawn for this work for which receipts should be given.

Area Commandants should be asked to send a representative to inspect camps the day the units move out.

O.C. Units will obtain a certificate from incoming units that they have taken over the camps in good order.

ACKNOWLEDGE.

B.H.Q.
29.12.17.

                                            Captain,
                                    Staff Captain,
                           199th Infantry Brigade.

                                               P.T.O.

DISTRIBUTION:-

Copy No. 1.....G.O.C.
"   "   2.....Brigade Major.
"   "   3.....Staff Captain.
"   "   4.....Bde.Sig.Officer.
"   "   5.....2/5th Manch.Regt.
"   "   6.....2/6th   "   "
"   "   7.....2/7th   "   "
"   "   8.....2/8th   "   "
"   "   9.....204th M.G.Coy.
"   " 10.....199th L.T.M.B.
"   " 11.....544 Coy. A.S.C.
"   " 12.....2/3rd Field Amb.
"   " 13.....Q.M. 2/5th Manch.R.
"   " 14.....Q.M. 2/6th   "   "
"   " 15.....Q.M. 2/7th   "   "
"   " 16.....Q.M. 2/8th   "   "
"   " 17.....36th Division, "Q"
"   " 18.....36th   "   "A"
"   " 19.....49th Division.
"   " 20.....New Zealand Division.
"   " 21.....Area Commandant, RENINGHELST.
"   " 22.....   "   "   CAESTRE.
"   " 23.....O.C, 36th Divisional Train.
"   " 24.....C.R.E.
"   " 25.....War Diary.
"   " 26.....   "   "
"   " 27.....File.
"   " 28.....Spare.
"   " 29..... "
"   " 30.....2/2nd Field Amb.
"   " 31.....Area Commandant, HALIFAX CAMP.

TABLE "A"

MOVE OF TRANSPORT

Transport of units will move independently as shown below:-

Transport of	30th Dec.	31st Dec.	1st Jan.
199 Bde. HQ.	-	To BOESCHEPE Area (West).	TO CAESTRE.
2/5th Manch.R.	To BOESCHEPE Area (West).	To BORRE.	-
2/6th " "	-	To BOESCHEPE Area (West)	HAZEBROUCK.
2/7th " "	-	To BOESCHEPE Area (West)	ST. SYLVESTRE CAPPEL.
2/8th " "	To BOESCHEPE Area (West).	To CAESTRE.	-
544 Coy. Div.Train.	To BOESCHEPE Area (West).	To BORRE.	-

A mounted advanced party from each unit concerned will apply to the Area Commandant, BOESCHEPE for accommodation, atvleast three hours before the unit arrives.
There will be no restrictions as to times of starting and routes.

T A B L E "C"

LORRIES FOR BAGGAGE.

Date.	Lorries required.	To report at.	Time.	Unit requiring them and purpose.
31st Dec.	3 lorries.	3 to report to 2/5th Manch.R. at BUSSEBOOM. 3 to report to 2/8th Manch.R. POPEREAL CAMP.	2 p.m. 2 p.m.	2/5th & 2/8th Manch.R. for conveyance of kit to BORRE and CAESTRE respectively.
1st Jan.	8 lorries.	5 to report H.Q. 2/3th Manch.R. G.22.b.5.4. 5 to report H.Q. 2/7th Manch.R. H.19.b.2.5. 2 to report Bde.H.Q. REMINGHELST.	2 p.m.	For conveyance of kit to HAZEBROUCK, ST.SILVESTRE CAPPEL and CAESTRE respectively.

TABLE "B"

SUPPLY ARRANGEMENTS DURING MOVE.

Unit.	Date.	Supplies (as concerning unit)	Remarks.
2/5th March.R. 2/8th " " 544 Coy A.S.C.	29th " "	Afternoon refill for consumption 30th. Transport moves on 30th with 2 days supplies, i.e. for consumption 30th and 31st. (See Note A.). Unconsumed portion ration for 31st to be carried on man when embussing. Train Transport will deliver rations direct to above units on 1st Jan. for consumption on 2nd Jan. On and after 2nd Jan. supplies will be drawn by 1st line transport at refilling point.	Note A. 1 wagon G.S. will be detailed from Train Coys. to report to each unit day prior to its transport moving to carry second days supplies for transport and personnel moving by road. These wagons will march with regtl. transport and report to Train Coy. immediately on arrival in new area. Note B. Only supplies will be loaded on these wagons.
H.Q. 190th Inf.Bde. 2/6th March.R. 2/7th "	30th " "	Transport moves 31st with 2 days supplies i.e. for consumption 31st and 1st (See Note A) Unconsumed portion ration for 31st to be carried on man when embussing. Train transport will deliver rations direct to above units on 1st Jan. for consumption on 2nd. On and after 2nd Jan. supplies will be drawn by 1st line transport at refilling point.	

II

Short Summary of events for the month

WAR DIARY
INTELLIGENCE SUMMARY.
(Erase heading not required.)

Army Form C. 2118.

During the month of December the 199th L.T.M.B. was not in the CAESTRE area. Training was carried out during the period. On Dec 16th the battalions of the Brigade left this area for 100% on the construction of trenches behind our line in front of YPRES. The 199th L.T.M.By. however remained behind. On Dec 31st the Battalion returned to the CAESTRE area. A few men were sent to the 199th L.T.M.Bty during the month, owing to chills etc. on account of the extremely cold weather.

Nothing of importance took place during the month.

Dec 31st 1917.

Kenneth Maiben Capt.
O.C. 199th L.T.M.B.

Army Form W.3091.

Cover for Documents.

Nature of Enclosures.

CONFIDENTIAL   ORIGINAL

WAR DIARY

of

199th L.T.M. BATTERY

FROM

1st Jan – 31st Jan 1918

VOLUME VI

Notes, or Letters written.

APPENDIX

I. T.P.R's
II. OPERATION ORDERS
III. Casualty Returns
IV. Short Summary of events for the month

Army Form C. 2118.

WAR DIARY
or
INTELLIGENCE SUMMARY.

(Erase heading not required.)

Instructions regarding War Diaries and Intelligence Summaries are contained in F. S. Regs., Part II. and the Staff Manual respectively. Title pages will be prepared in manuscript.

Place	Date	Hour	Summary of Events and Information	Remarks and references to Appendices
ST. SYLVESTRE CAPPEL (CAESTRE AREA)	1918 Jan 1st		Weather fine. Training. S.&.q.	
"	" 2nd		Weather fine. Training. S.&.q.	
"	" 3rd		Weather fine. Training. S.&.q.	
"	" 4th		Weather fair. Training. S.&.q.	
"	" 5th		Weather wet. Training. R.C. Battalion went to Church Parade S.&.q. 10.10. S.&.q.	
"	" 6th		Weather unsettled. Church Parade. S.&.q.	Before div. Copy to 10.
"	" 7th		Snow. The Divisional Recreation hut Set. Bruille R.O.O. to 73 Copy to 10	R.O.O. 73
"	" 8th		Weather wet. Training Ref. R.O.O. B.O.O. 74 Copy to 10 + Admin. Ollr. No. 34 S.&.q	R.O.O. 74 Admin 34
"	" 9th		Weather unsettled. O.S. Insts #9 (with lists) of the 146th S.T.M.B. to arrange S.&.q.	
"	" 10th		Ruled Training S.&.q.	
"	" 11th		Weather wet. Training. Training up to work. S.&.q. Ruenile R.O.O. to 75 Copy to 11.	B.O.O. 75

Army Form C. 2118.

WAR DIARY
or
INTELLIGENCE SUMMARY.
(Erase heading not required.)

Instructions regarding War Diaries and Intelligence Summaries are contained in F. S. Regs., Part II. and the Staff Manual respectively. Title pages will be prepared in manuscript.

Place	Date	Hour	Summary of Events and Information	Remarks and references to Appendices
ST SYLVESTRE CAPPEL (CAESTRE AREA)	1918 Jan 11		The Battery marched out from Billets @ 7-45 a.m. to the CAESTRE-ST. SYLVESTRE-CAPPEL Road where it embussed in accordance with B.6.0.no 74. It debussed just north of KRUISTRAAT and marched into the POTIJZE AREA where it remained for the night. Weather fine.	
POTIJZE AREA	" 12		The Battery marched to Brasserie @ 10-15 a.m. and relieved the 146 F.S.T.M.B. in the BROODSEINDE RIDGE SECTOR. Relief completed without casualties @ 1-45 p.m. Weather fine.	T.P.R 12/1/18-13/1/18
BROODSEINDE RIDGE SECTOR	" 13		Weather fine. Our guns were quiet.	T.P.R 13/1/18-14/1/18
"	" 14		Ensue. Our guns were quiet.	

Army Form C. 2118.

WAR DIARY
or
INTELLIGENCE SUMMARY.

(Erase heading not required.)

Instructions regarding War Diaries and Intelligence Summaries are contained in F. S. Regs., Part II. and the Staff Manual respectively. Title pages will be prepared in manuscript.

Place	Date	Hour	Summary of Events and Information	Remarks and references to Appendices
BROODSEINDE RIDGE SECTOR	1918. Jan 15th		Snow. Our guns were quiet. S.E.Q.	T.P.R 14/1/18 – 15/1/18.
"	" 16th		Weather wet. Quiet. S.E.Q.	T.P.R 15/1/18 – 16/1/18.
"	" 17th		Weather fine. Quiet. S.E.Q.	T.P.R 16/1/18 – 17/1/18.
"	" 18th		Weather fine. Received O.O. No. 76 copy No. 5. No. 1 Section relieved by No. III Relief complete without enemy activity by 11.30 a.m. S.E.Q.	T.P.R 17/1/18 – 18/1/18. O.O. No.76 18/1/18 T.P.R 18/1/18 – 19/1/18.
"	" 19		Weather unsettled. Dull. S.E.Q.	T.P.R 19/1/18 – 19/1/18.
"	" 20.30		Weather wet. Received Amm. Order No. 55 copy No. 18 also B.M. order No 77 copy No.10.	Amm.O. No.55 A.O.O No.77 T.P.R 19/1/18 – 20/1/18.
"	" 21st		Weather fine. Officer from 195th S.T.M.B. visited our H.Q. in the line to arrange relief. Quiet.	T.P.R 20/1/18 – 21/1/18.
"	22		Weather fine. The Battery were relieved in the line by the 195th S.T.M.B. and marched into Huts @ HALIFAX CAMP. Relief complete 2 p.m. Arrived HALIFAX CAMP 6.30 p.m.	T.P.R 21/1/18 – 22/1/18.

Army Form C. 2118.

WAR DIARY
or
INTELLIGENCE SUMMARY.
(Erase heading not required.)

Instructions regarding War Diaries and Intelligence Summaries are contained in F.S. Regs., Part II. and the Staff Manual respectively. Title pages will be prepared in manuscript.

Place	Date	Hour	Summary of Events and Information	Remarks and references to Appendices
HALIFAX CAMP.	1918 April 23		Weather fine. Training &c.	
"	" 24		Weather fine. Training &c.	
"	" 25		Weather fine. Training &c.	
"	" 26		Weather fine. Training &c. Rec'd B.O.O.no78 & by W10 K.O.O min. O.no36	B.O.O.no78 Admin O.no 36
"	" 27		Weather fine. Church Parade. O.C. 199 & 2nd F.B. visit to O.C.119T wilt Genl to arrange relief.	
E.F.T ZONNEBEKE SECTOR.	" 28		Weather fine. Relief was carried out in accordance with B.O.O.no78. No 2 Section Relief complete 12.30 p.m. No 1 Section marched to POTIJZE CAMP arriving there @ 5-15 p.m.	
"	" 29		Weather fine. Quiet. Enemy Artillery activity. Lt. J.S. MAYER killed by enemy shell.	

Army Form C. 2118.

WAR DIARY
or
INTELLIGENCE SUMMARY.
(Erase heading not required.)

Place	Date	Hour	Summary of Events and Information	Remarks and references to Appendices
LEFT ZONNEBEKE SECTOR	1918 Jan 30th		Weather fine. Normal.	29/1/18 – 30/1/18.
"	31st	1.31	Weather fine. LT: J.S. MAYER buried @ MENIN RD. CEMETRY.	30/1/18 – 31/1/18.

T.P.R's

Daily Tactical Progress Report
From 6 a.m. 12.1.'18 to 6 a.m. 13.1.'18.
Unit. COD.

1) Operations.

Our guns were inactive. They report that the front was quiet throughout the night

Sheppard Lieut.
o.c.
"COD"

Daily Tactical Progress Report.

From 6 am. 13.1.18 to 6 am. 14.1.18.

Unit "COD"

A. Operations.

Our guns were inactive. The past 24 hours were uneventful.

[signature] Lieut
o.c.
"COD"

Daily Tactical Progress Report

From 6 am. 14.1.'18 to 6 am. 15.1.'18

Unit:- "COD"

A. Operations

Our guns were inactive. The past 24 hours were uneventful.

Stopdall Lieut.
O.C.
"COD"

Daily Tactical Progress Report

From 6am. 15.1.'18. to 6am 16.1.'18

Unit "COD".

A. **Operations.** Our guns inactive. The front was quiet throughout the day.

S. Cryscall Lieut
O.C.
"COD"

Daily Tactical Progress Report

From 6 a.m. 16.1.'18 to 6 a.m. 17.1.'18.

Unit:- "C O D"

A. **Operations:-** Our guns were inactive. The front was quiet throughout the day.

                                                S. Goodall Lieut
                                                           O.C.
                                                           "C O D"

Daily Tactical Progress Report
From 6 am 17.1.'18 to 6 am 18.1.'18.

Unit :- COD.

9. Operations :-   Our guns still inactive.
Extreme quietness prevailed along the front.

                                                    [signature] Lieut
                                                                O.C.
                                                                'COD'

Daily Tactical Progress Report.
From 6am. 18.1.18 to 6am. 19.1.18.

Unit:- COD.

A. Operations.

Our guns still inactive. Slight increase in Enemy artillery activity during the afternoon. Situation otherwise quiet.

S.P. Goodall Lieut.
for O.C.
"COD"

Daily Tactical Progress Report.
From 6am. 19·1·'18 to 6am. 20·1·'18

Unit: "COD"

A. Operations:— At 2·30pm. our Stokes fired a burst at a low flying enemy aeroplane. The aeroplane remained over our lines for half an hour but kept out of range of our guns.

Leopold Lieut.
O.C.
COD.

Daily Tactical Progress Report.
From 6 a.m. 20.1.'18 to 6 a.m. 21.1.'18

Unit: "C O D"

Operations:- Our guns inactive.

S. Lyptall Lieut.
o.c.
COD

Daily Tactical Progress Report

From 6 a.m. 21.1.18 to 6 a.m. 22.1.18.

Unit:- COD

Operations:- Our guns engaged one E.A. at about 4.20 p.m. causing it to return over its own lines.

Shepard Lieut
O.C.
COD

Daily Tactical Progress Report

Unit: "C O D"
From 6am. 28.1.'18. to 6am. 29.1.'18

A. Operations.

Our guns were quiet owing to relief.

S.C. Goodall Lieut
for O.C.
"COD"

Daily Tactical Progress Report

Unit "COD"
From 6am 29.1.'18 to 6am 30.1.18

A. Operations.
   Our guns inactive.
Enemy artillery very active.

2/Lt Lieut
for o.c.
"COD"

Daily Tactical Progress Report.

Unit COD.
From 6am 30.1.'18 to 6am 31.1.18.

A Operations. Our guns still inactive. The front was quiet throughout the day.

S.C. Yoxall Lieut
for O.C.
COD

II

Operation Orders

SECRET.   Copy No... 10

199th Infantry Brigade
PRELIMINARY ORDER.

1. The 199th Infantry Brigade will move from the CAESTRE sub-area on Jan.11th. into the POTIJZE area, and will relieve the 146th Infantry Brigade in the Line, Right Sub-sector, on the night 12/13th January, (See March Table A attached).

2. The 204th Machine Gun Coy. will move to the forward area with the Brigade Group, but reliefs of the front line Companies will take place on the night following the Infantry relief.
   All details for relief will be arranged by the D.M.G.O. who will issue separate orders.

3. 2/3rd Field Ambulance move with Brigade Group on 11th, and relieve 1/1st W.R.Fld.Amb. at WARATAH CAMP near POPERINGHE.

4. (a) The extreme importance of the position which the Division is about to take over, and the necessity for the most vigorous action in the event of a temporary hostile success, must be impressed on all ranks.

   (b) The whole of the front line system is to be held at all costs. If the enemy does succeed in penetrating into any part of our positions, he is to be ejected at once by immediate local counter-attack.

5. ACKNOWLEDGE.

                                                          Captain,
                                                          A/Brigade Major,
B.H.Q.   199th Infantry Brigade.
5.1.18.

Distribution:-

Copy No,1....G.O.C.
  "   "   2....Brigade Major,
  "   "   3....Staff Captain,
  "   "   4....Bde.Signal Officer.
  "   "   5....O.C, 2/5th Manch.Regt.
  "   "   6....O.C, 2/6th   "   "
  "   "   7....O.C, 2/7th   "   "
  "   "   8....O.C, 2/8th   "   "
  "   "   9....O.C, 204th M.G.Coy.
  "   " 10....O.C, 199th L.T.M.B.
  "   " 11....O.C, 2/3rd Field Amb.
  "   " 12....O.C, 544 Coy.A.S.C.
  "   " 13....War Diary.
  "   " 14.... "   "
  "   " 15....File.
  "   " 16....Spare.
  "   " 17.... "

P.T.O.

MARCH TABLE A.

Serial No.	Date.	Unit.	From.	To.	Route etc.	Remarks.
1.	Jan.10th.	Transport of 199th Bde. Group.	CAESTRE Sub-area.	TIPPENHOEK (Staging area)	CAESTRE-GODEWAERS-VELDE - ABEELE	To clear CAESTRE by 10 a.m.
2.	" 11th.	199th Bde. Group.	"	POTIJZE area.	By bus.	
3.	" 11th.	Serial No.1.	TIPPENHOEK area.	Transport lines of 143th Bde.	By road. No restrictions.	
4.	" 12th.	199th Bde. Group. (less F.C.C)	POTIJZE area.	Line. Right Sub-sector.	—	Relieving 143th Inf. Bde. on night 12/13th Jan.

NOTES. (a) Field Coy. R.E. are NOT included in Brigade Groups.
(b) Arrangements for advance billeting parties for TIPPENHOEK and forward areas will be notified by "Q" Branch later

SECRET.   Copy No. 10

199th Infantry Brigade
OPERATION ORDER No. 73.

Ref: Sheets 27S.E. & 28. 1/40,000.

1. The 199th Infantry Brigade Group will move on January 10th and 11th as laid down in Brigade "Preliminary" Order of 5.1.18.

2. Movement Table to follow.

3. Details for the relief of 204th Machine Gun Coy. have been issued under Divisional order 529/18 G. of 4.1.18.

4. "Code Names" and "Station Code Calls" will be taken into use on arrival in the forward area.

5. Careful records with receipts will be kept of all documents, equipment and stores taken over.

6. Particular attention is called to Fourth Army GS.148 issued under this Office No.G.640 of 28.12.17.

7. Before leaving area units should arrange to collect and store as near the work as possible, all loose wood, corrugated iron and other material which might be removed by the inhabitants during the time the area is unoccupied.

8. Guides will be detailed from the advance party to meet units at debussing point at 10.30 a.m.

    Road North of Kruisstraat from H.18.d.9.8.
    to H.18.d.4.8.

to guide units to the billets in POTIJZE.

9. Brigade Headquarters will close at CAESTRE at 9.30 a.m. 11.1.18. and reopen on arrival at Infantry Barracks, YPRES.

10. ACKNOWLEDGE.

B.H.Q.
7.1.18.

Captain,
A/Brigade Major,
199th Infantry Brigade.

Distribution:-

Copy No. 1.....G.O.C.
"   "   2.....Brigade Major.
"   "   3.....Staff Captain.
"   "   4.....Bde. Signal Officer.
"   "   5.....2/5th Lanch.Regt.
"   "   6.....2/6th   "   "
"   "   7.....2/7th   "   "
"   "   8.....2/8th   "   "
"   "   9.....204th Machine Gun Coy.
"   "   10.....199th L.T.M.Battery.
"   "   11.....2/3rd Field Amb.
"   "   12.....544 Coy. A.S.C.
"   "   13.....66th Division, "G"
"   "   14.....66th   "   "A"
War Li 15.....War Diary.
"   "   16.....   "   "
"   "   17.....File.
"   "   18.....Spare.

SECRET.   Copy No. 10

199th Infantry Brigade
OPERATION ORDER No. 74.

Ref: Sheets 27 S.E. and 28 - 1/40,000.

1. Attached is movement table referred to in Brigade Operation Order No. 73.

2. Brigade Signalling Officer will arrange for signalling classes to be continued behind the lines while Brigade is in the trenches. Full details will be issued later by the Brigade Signalling Officer, and this personnel will be left behind by units in the POTIJZE Area, and then proceed to their respective Transport Lines.

3. Undermentioned personnel to be cut down to absolutely necessary minimum by C.O.s. of front line and Support Battalion.

    Signallers.
    Runners.
    Lewis Gunners.

Surplus personnel to be accommodated behind the line.

4. ACKNOWLEDGE.

                                                Captain,
                                                A/Brigade Major,
                                                199th Infantry Brigade.

a.l.c.

Distribution:-

Copy No. 1.....G.O.C.
"   "   2.....Brigade Major,
"   "   3.....Staff Captain,
"   "   4.....Bde. Signal Officer.
"   "   5.....2/5th Manch. Regt.
"   "   6.....2/6th   "   "
"   "   7.....2/7th   "   "
"   "   8.....2/8th   "   "
"   "   9.....204th Machine Gun Coy.
"   "   10....199th L.T.M.B.
"   "   11....2/3rd Field Ambulance.
"   "   12....544 Coy. A.S.C.
"   "   13....66th Division, "Q"
"   "   14....66th   "   "A"
"   "   15....War Diary.
"   "   16.... "   "
"   "   17....File.
"   "   18....Spare.
"   "   19....

MOVEMENT TABLE - 199th INFANTRY BRIGADE.

Date.	Unit in order of embussing.	Embussing Point.	Times ready to embus.	Column moves.	Debussing Point.	Destination.	Number of busses.	REMARKS.
Jan. 7th.	204th M.G.C.	CAESTRE-ST.SILVESTRE CAPPEL Road. Column facing W. Head at G.31.b.5.4.	8.45 a.m.	9.30 a.m.	WARATAH CMP. G.15.c.2.9.	WARATAH CMP.	1 - 7.	C.Os. will detail guides from the advance parties to meet units at debussing points at 10.30 a.m. & guide them to their billeting area.
	199th L.T.M.B.		8.45 a.m.	9.30 a.m.			8 - 10.	
	2/6th Manch R		9.00 a.m.	"	Road north of KRUIS-STRAAT from H.13.d.9.6. To I.12.d.3.4.6.	POTIJZE AREA.	11 - 37.	
	2/7th "		9.00 a.m.	"			38 - 61.	
	2/8th "		8.45 a.m.	"			62 - 91.	
	2/5th "		9.00 a.m.	"			92 - 121	
	Bde.H.Q.		9.00 a.m.	"			122 - 126	
	2/3rd Fld.Art. (dismounted portion.)	Rue d'Eglise HAZEBROUCK.	8.30 a.m.	9.00 a.m.	WARATAH CMP. G.15.c.2.9.	WARATAH CMP.	Six.	

SECRET.   Copy No.....
                              199th Infantry Brigade
                              ADMINISTRATIVE ORDER
                                    No.84.
                              ─────────

                          Ref: Sheet 28 N.W.

MOVE.   The 199th Infantry Brigade Group will relieve the 14th
                 Infantry Brigade Group as laid down in Brigade Preliminary
                 Order of 7.1.18.

BILLETING   Billeting Parties will report at Brigade H.Q. at 7.45 a.m.
PARTIES.   on the 10th inst. as under :-

                          Brigade Headquarters   5.
                          2/5th, 2/6th, 2/7th
                          and 2/8th March R.   6 each.
                          204th M.G.Coy. 2/3rd
                          Field Amb. and 199th
                          L.T.M.Battery.   3 each.

                 Parties from the Field Ambulance and Machine Gun Coy. will
                 report at WARATAH CAMP (1/1st W.R.Fld.Amb.) G.15.c.2.9.
                 Remainder will report to Area Commandant, POTIJZE Area
                 (1.4.c.8.5.) for accommodation for Units arriving next day.
                 Rations for the 11th. to be taken.
                 Accommodation for night 10/11th. will be provided by Area
                 Commandant, POTIJZE Area.

TRANSPORT.   Transport will move off independently at following times :-

                          B.H.Q.   7.45 a.m.
                          2/8th March R.   8.00 a.m.
                          204th M.G.Coy.   8.30 a.m.
                          2/7th March R.   8.45 a.m.
                          2/6th   "   "   9.00 a.m.
                          2/5th   "   "   9.15 a.m.

                 Mounted advance parties from all Units staying in the
                 WIPPENHOEK Area will report at least three hours before
                 the arrival of the Transport to Lt.-Col. MULLINER, Area
                 Commandant, WIPPENHOEK.

BAGGAGE &   Baggage and supply wagons will report to Units on the day
SUPPLY WAGONS.   previous to the move of Transport.

LORRIES.   Lorries for the conveyance of baggage will report at B.HKQ.
                 CAESTRE, at 7 a.m. 11th inst. and will be allotted as follows:-

                          B.H.Q.   2.
                          2/5th March R   3.
                          2/6th   "   "   3.
                          2/7th   "   "   2.
                          2/8th   "   "   2.
                          204th M.G.Coy.   1.
                          199th L.T.M.B.   1.

                 1 lorry each for 2/7th and 2/8th will do two journeys
                 if required.

GUIDES.   Guides for lorries will report at Staff Captain's Office,
                 CAESTRE, at 6.45 a.m. A Guide for each unit from billeting
                 party will be sent back to his unit in CAESTRE area on
                 reaching BELGIAN CHATEAU on the 10th inst, so that he can
                 personally conduct lorries to his own Q.M.Stores at BELGIAN
                 CHATEAU on the 11th inst. Billeting parties will send a
                 guide from POTIJZE Area on the 11th inst. to meet lorries
                 arriving at Q.M.Stores at 10 a.m. These guides will conduct
                 lorries or baggage wagons to the POTIJZE area if necessary.

(2).

TRANSPORT LOCATIONS ON COMPLETION OF MOVES.

Unit.	Locality.	Date of taking over.	Relieving.
109th T.M.B.	H.23.a.3.9.		Corresponding units of 146th Inf.Bde.
A Battalion.	H.23.a.3.9.		
B "	H.23.a.3.9.	Jan. 11th.	
C "	H.23.c.4.5.		
D "	H.23.b.8.5.		
204th M.G.Coy.	H.18.c.4.3.	" 13th.	Lines of 254th M.G.Coy.
No. 4 Coy, Div. Train.	G.32.a.9.9.	" 11th.	No.2 Coy.49/Div. Train.
2/3rd Fld.Amb. and transport.	G.15.c.8.9. (WARATAH CAMP) POPERINGHE.	" 11th.	1/1 W.R.Fld.Amb.
Mobile Vet. Section.	G.34.b.7.9.	" 12th.	49th Div. M.V. Section.
ORDNANCE OFFICE & Workshops.	RENINGHELST.	" 13th.	49/Div.Ordnance.

AREA STORES IN BACK AREA.
All Area Stores on charge of Units in the back area will be collected together prior to departure and handed over to the Area Commandant, from whom receipts will be obtained. Copies of these receipts will be forwarded to D.H.Q. by the 13th inst.

TRENCH STORES & AREA STORES IN 49th DIV AREA.
1. All reserve supplies, ammunition, trench and area stores, will be carefully checked before being taken over, and receipts will be given. Copies of all receipts will be forwarded to D.H.Q. by the 14th inst.
2. Pack Saddlery. will be handed over by the 49th Division, and will be drawn from Brigade H.Q.Transport Lines.

SOLIDIFIED ALCOHOL.
Solidified alcohol will be issued under Brigade arrangements to the two Q.M.Stores of the two Battalions in the line and the 204th M.G.Coy. on Jan. 11th.

TRENCH FOOT.
(a) Attention is called to 63th Divn. letter No.2451/A dated 13th Dec.1917. It is most important that every man's foot are carefully washed and treated as laid down in the above quoted letter before going into the trenches.

(b) Socks. Every man going into the trenches must be in possession of two pairs of socks in addition to those he is wearing. The 49th Divn. have agreed to units of this Divn. in the line exchanging socks at the 49th Div. YPRES, in a similar manner to their own Units.
The following procedure adopted by the 49th Divn. will be carried out by Units of this Divn. until other arrangements can be made.
Every day the socks of all men in the line will be changed the discarded socks being put into sandbags – 1 sandbag to each platoon.
One man per platoon (or an equivalent number of men per battn) will carry the sandbags of dirty socks to the 49th Divn. Baths, YPRES, and there receive a similar number of clean dry socks.

(3).

TRENCH FOOT (Continued)	(c) <u>Foot troughs</u>. In the camps occupied by the 4 Battalions of the Reserve Brigade and the Reserve Battalions of Brigade in the line, there are two troughs for foot washing and two Soyer stoves. These will be taken over and used.
	(d) <u>Trench foot powder and soap</u>. This will be drawn from Brigade Q.M.Stores on the 12th inst.
ORDNANCE.	On and after Jan.15th. Brigade will ddawn from D.A.D.O.S. Store, RENINGHELST.
SUPPLY ARRANGEMENTS.	The following table shows the Supply arrangements during the move.
	Refilling Points for units on first arrival in the new area are being reechroitred and will be notified direct to units by O.C. Div. Train.
	When the relief of the 49th Division has been completed refilling point will be H.19.b.5.5.

Supply arrangements.

Date.	Unit or Formtn.	Refills.	Consumption on.	Remarks.
Jan.9th.	199th Inf.Bde. Group.	8.30 a.m.	Jan.10th.	From present dump.
" 9th	199th Inf.Bde. group plus certain details.	3 p.m.	Jan.11th.	" " "
" 11th.	199th Inf.Bde. Group.	On arrival in new area.	Jan.12th.	By Train transport.
" 12th.	" " "	9 a.m.	Jan.13th.	By 1st line transport and daily until further notice.

RUNNERS.	As soon as Transport and Q.M.Stores have been fixed up in BELGIAN CHATEAU area, units will send the following runners to Brigade Rear H.Q. Infantry Barracks, YPRES, to report to Staff Captain.

199th B.H.Q.	2.
2/5th March R.	2.
2/6th " "	2.
2/7th " "	2.
2/8th " "	2.
204th M.G.Coy.	1.
199th L.T.M.B.	1.

AMMUNITION.	This can be drawn on demand from the Bomb Stores shown below. There is no need to indent on Brigade H.Q.

Left draw from GARTER POINT.
MOULIN FARM.
Right " " GARTER POINT.

R.E.MATERIAL.	This can be drawn on indent to N.C.O. in charge of dump as follows :-

Left......MOULIN FARM.
RIGHT.....YORKSHIRE DUMP.

RATIONS & WATER. Personnel of front line companies will not be sent back to the dump to carry up rations or water.
The necessary carrying parties will be obtained from the following sources:-
(a) Battalion H.Q. Personnel. (b) Surplus men not employed in the line (c) Available of transport personnel (d) Support and Reserve Battalions.

Commanding Officers will ensure that Transport Officers and Q.Ms. are fully acquainted with the procedure being adopted and the position of tracks and dumps.
The Battalion Q.M. or Q.M.S. will accompany rations to the forward dump and hand them over. When transshipment from wheel to pack transport has to take place at night, it is desirable to have the loads roped up beforehand at the Q.M.Stores or Transport Lines.

J.S. Fox Captain,
Staff Captain,
199th Infantry Brigade.

B.H.Q.
8.1.18.

Distribution:-

Copy No. 1.... G.O.C.
"   "   2.... Brigade Major.
"   "   3.... Staff Captain.
"   "   4.... Bde. Sig. Officer.
"   "   5.... O.C. 2/5th Manch R.
"   "   6.... "   2/6th "   "
"   "   7.... "   2/7th "   "
"   "   8.... "   2/8th "   "
"   "   9.... 204th M.G.Coy.
"   "   10.... 199th L.T.M.B.
"   "   11.... 544 Coy A.S.C.
"   "   12.... 2/3rd Fld.Amb.
"   "   13.... Q.M. 2/5th Manch.R.
"   "   14.... Q.M. 2/6th   "   "
"   "   15.... "   2/7th   "   "
"   "   16.... "   2/8th   "   "
"   "   17.... Area Commandant, CAESTRE.
"   "   18....   "   "   POTIJZE Area.
"   "   19.... 66th Divnl.Train.
"   "   20.... 66th Division, "G"
"   "   21.... "   "   "A"
"   "   22.... 49th   "   "A"
"   "   23.... War Diary.
"   "   24.... "   "
"   "   25.... File.
"   "   26.... Spare.
"   "   27.... "

Acknowledge.

SECRET.

Copy No. 10

199th Infantry Brigade
OPERATION ORDER No. 75.

1. The 199th Infantry Brigade will relieve the 146th Infantry Brigade in the line, right subsector on Jan.12th.

2. The 204th M.G.Coy. will relieve the 146th M.G.Coy. on the night of Jan.13/14th. as laid down in 66th Divn.Order 529/18 G.

3. C.O.s. of 2/5th, 2/6th & 2/8th Manch.R. will detail their 2nds in Command to proceed on the Motor Baggage Lorry on the morning of the 11th, and they will report at the 146th Bde. H.Q. D.26.c.1.3. They will then proceed to the Headquarters of the Unit they are relieving, and obtain full information of the strength of all posts, and maximum accommodation, take over details of all work in progress, reports required, etc. These officers will return to their units tomorrow night at POTIJZE and complete arrangements for their Battalion relief.

4. One officer per each front line Company and 1 per Batt. H.Q. in the line, will be left behind by the 146th Bde. These 6 officers will remain for 24 hours, and then report to 2/7th Manch.Regt. DRAGOON CAMP who will accommodate these officers on the night 13/14th. January.

5. O.C. 2/7th Manch.Regt. will detail daily commencing 13th. 1 N.C.O. and 3 men (with Lewis Gun and ammunition) to take over A.A.Post at Brigade Headquarters. This is mounted at 6.45 a.m. and dismounted at 4 p.m.

6. Brigade Headquarters will close at Infantry Barracks, YPRES, at 3 p.m. and reopen at D.26.c.1.3. on arrival.

7. Completion of relief to be reported by code word "HAPPY"

8. ACKNOWLEDGE.

10.1.18.

Captain,
A/Brigade Major,
199th Infantry Brigade.

Distribution:-

Copy No. 1....G.O.C.	Copy No. 12...2/3rd Fld.Amb.
" " 2....Brigade Major,	" " 13...544 Coy.A.S.C.
" " 3....Staff Captain,	" " 14...66th Div. "G"
" " 4....Bde.Sig.Officer.	" " 15...66th " "A"
" " 5....2/5th Manch.R.	" " 16...49th " "G"
" " 7....2/6th " "	" " 17...146th Inf.Bde.
" " 8....2/7th " "	" " 18...War Diary,
" " 9....2/8th " "	" " 19..." "
" " 10....204th M.G.Coy.	" " 20...File.
" " 11....199th L.T.M.B.	" " 21...Spare.
	" " 22..."

MOVEMENT TABLE TO ACCOMPANY BRIGADE OPERATION ORDER No. 35.

Date.	Unit.	From.	To.	Relieving.	Guides 1 per platoon 1 " Batt HQ. meet at	Remarks.
Jan.12th.	2/5th W.R.	POTIJZE.	Line (Left Sector).	1/5th W.York R.	Junction of Cambridge Rd & Zonnebeke Rd. I.5.a. 25/70. 3.0 p.m.	1 officer to be sent to DRAGOON CMP.on arvl. to take over all accommdtn. Arrangements for relief to be made between C.Os. concerned. Relief to be complete by 2 p.m. 12.1.18.
"	2/8th W.R.	"	" Right Sector.	1/8th "	Junction of Mule Track & Cambridge Rd. I.11.b.1.7. 3.0 p.m.	
"	2/5th W.R.	"	Support.	1/5th "	Junction of POTIJZE -Cambridge Rd. 11 a.m.	
"	2/7th W.R.	"	Reserve.	1/7th "	"	Details of relief C.Os concerned to complete by 2 p.m.
"	69th LTM.B.	"	"	146th L.T.M.B.		Details of relief to be arranged C.Os. concerned
" 13/14.	204th M.G.C.	"	"	146th M.G.Coy.		

NOTE:- Rendezvous for guides should be previously reconnoitred
usual distances between Platoons.

SECRET　　　　　　　　　　　　　　　　　　　　No 5.

199 INFANTRY BDE.,
OPERATION ORDER No 76

1. The inter-Battalion relief will take place on the night of JAN, 18/19th as per warning order BM 40, and attached TABLE "A".

2. All details of the times of relief and guides etc., to be made between C.O's concerned.

3. Defence Schemes, Maps, Trench stores and full details of all working parties will be handed over, and all work must be carried on without interruption, and parties kept up to full strength exclusive of supervising Officers and N.C.O's.

4. Completion of relief will be reported by code word SMILE.

5. One Officer per each front line company will be left behind by the 2/5 & 2/7 Man. Regt for 24 hours.

H. Bon. Capt.
Brigade Major
TROUT

No 1 TO O/C 2/5 MAN REGT
No 2 "   "   2/6
No 3 "   "   2/7
No 4 "   "   2/8
No 5 "   "   LTMB
No 6 "   "   204 M.G.Coy
No 7   G.O.C
No 8   STAFF CAPT
No 9   BDE SIGNALS
No 10   66 DY.
No 11   197 INF BDE
No 12   3RD N.Z. BDE.
No 13   SPARE
No 14   FILE
No 15   FILE
No 16   WAR DIARY
No 17   "   "

TABLE "A" TO ACCOMPANY 3rd BRIGADE OPERATION ORDER No. 76

DATE	UNIT	FROM	TO	RELIEVING	REMARKS
JAN 13	2 MAN R	OUT LINE R (2nd COMPANY)	LINE R	26 MAN REGT	ON RELIEF 2.8 MAN REGT PASSED TO 49TH BDE. TO CENTRAL
	2 MAN R	SUPPORT LINE LEFT		28 MAN REGT	ON RELIEF 28 MAN REGT PASSED TO BUSSEQ(?)
	L.T.M.B. 3 MAN REGT				J3 & 5
	3rd H.Q. C.S.				

SECRET.

Copy No. 10

199th. Infantry Brigade
ADMINISTRATIVE ORDER NO. 55.

Reference :- Sheet 28 N.W.

RELIEF. The 199th. Infantry Brigade, less 204th.M.G.Coy., will be relieved on January 22/23rd. 1918, by the 198th. Inf. Brigade.

BILLETS. Billets will be taken over from the outgoing Brigade as follows :-

199th. B.H.Q.	from	198th. B.H.Q.	HALIFAX Camp.
2/5th.Lanc.Regt.	"	2/9th.Lanc.Regt	H.Q.BELGIAN CHAU. CANAL AREA H.18.c.3.1.
2/6th.Lanc.Regt.	"	2/4th.E.Lancs.R.	HALIFAX Camp H.14.c.8.5
2/7th.Lanc.Regt.	"	2/10th.Lanc.Regt.	VANCOUVER Camp H.14.b.2.7
2/8th.Lanc.Regt.	"	2/5th.E.Lanc.Regt.	INFANTRY BARRACKS YPRES.
199th.L.T.M.B.	"	198th.L.T.M.B.	HALIFAX CAMP.

BILLETING PARTIES. Units will arrange for Billeting Parties to inspect their respective locations on the 21st. inst. and make necessary arrangements for guiding Units into new Billets.

Q.M.STORES & TRANSPORT LINES. Q.M.Stores and Transport Lines, with the exception of B.H.Q. Q.M.Stores, will remain in present locations. Brigade Q.M. Stores will move to HALIFAX Camp to take over Stores occupied by 198th.Brigade.

SUPPLIES. As at present.

BAGGAGE WAGONS. Baggage Wagons will be at BELGIAN BATTERY Corner at 9 a.m. on 22nd. inst. Units will send Guides to conduct same to Q.M.Stores.

TRENCH & AREA STORES. All Trench and Area Stores will be handed over and receipts taken. Copies of receipts for Stores handed over and taken over will be forwarded to this Office by 12 noon 23rd. inst.

GUM BOOTS. All wet Gum Boots will be handed in to Infantry Barracks, YPRES.

ACKNOWLEDGE.

B.H.Q.
20-1-1918.

J.S. Fox Captain,
Staff Captain,
199th. Infantry Brigade.

P.T.O.

Distribution:-

Copy No.		
1.	G.O.C.	
2.	Brigade Major.	
3.	Staff Captain.	
4.	Bde.Sig.Officer.	
5.	O.C. 2/5th Lanc.R.	
6.	" 2/6th " "	
7.	" 2/7th " "	
8.	" 2/8th " "	
9.	" 204th M.G.Coy.	
10.	" 199th L.T.M.B.	
11.	" 544 Coy A.S.C.	
12.	" 2/3rd Fld.Amb.	
13.	O.C. 2/5th Lanc.Rgt.(Rear)	
14.	2/6th " " "	
15.	2/7th " " "	
16.	2/8th " " "	
17.	204th M.G.Coy. "	
18.	199th L.T.M.B. "	
19.	Area Commandant Potijze Area
20.	" " Canal Area
21.	" " Pioneer Area
22.	" " Halifax Area.
23.	66th Div. Train	
24.	66th Div A.	
25.	198th Infy Bde.	
26.	War Diary	
27.	" "	
28.	File	
29.	Spare.	

SECRET.

199th. Infantry Brigade
OPERATION ORDER NO.77.

Copy No. 10

Ref:- MAP. Sheet 28. 1/40,000,
           28. N.E.1. 1/10,000.

1. The 199th. Infantry Brigade will be relieved in the Line on January 22nd./23rd.

2. Relief will be in accordance with attached Table "A".

3. On relief, the 199th. Infantry Brigade will be in Divisional Reserve.

4. (a) There will be no cessation of work by this Brigade on the day of relief, and normal working parties will be furnished.

   (b) On January 23rd., working parties will be found in accordance with Table B (to be issued later).

5. One Officer per Company and One per Battalion H.Q. will be left behind with Units of 198th. Infantry Brigade for 24 hours. These Officers will then make their own way to rejoin their Units.

6. All Defence Schemes, details of work in progress and proposed, Trench Stores, Maps, Reports required, will be handed over and receipts obtained for documents, maps and stores.

7. Completion of relief to be reported by code word "CINCH".

8. Command will pass on completion of relief, and Brigade H.Q. will afterwards re-open at H.19.b.2.7.

9. ACKNOWLEDGE.

J.S. Fox
Captain,
Brigade Major,
199th. Infantry Brigade.

B.H.Q.
20.1.19.

Distribution:-
Copy No. 1 .... G.O.C.
         2 .... Brigade Major.
         3 .... Staff Captain.
         4 .... Bde. Signal Officer.
         5 .... 2/5th. Manc. Regt.
         6 .... 2/6th.   "   "
         7 .... 2/7th.   "   "
         8 .... 2/8th.   "   "
         9 .... 204th. M.G. Coy.
        10 .... 199th. L.T.M.B.
        11 .... 197th. Inf. Bde.
        12 .... 198th.   "   "
        13 .... 2nd. N.Z. Brigade.
        14 .... 66th. Division "G"
        15 ....   "A"
        16 .... War Diary.
        17 ....   "
        18 .... File.
        19 .... Spare.
        20 ....   "

TABLE "A" TO ACCOMPANY 199th. INFANTRY BRIGADE ORDER NO.77.

UNIT.	From	Relieved By	TO	Now Occupied By	Guides(1 per platoon 1 per Battn.H.Q.) meet 198th.Bde.Units	Remarks.
2/7th. Manc.Regt.(Right)	LIFE	2/5th. E/Lancs.Regt.	VANCOUVER E.14.b.7.7	2/10th. Manc.Regt.	Junc.of Mule Track and CAMBRIDGE Road. I.11.b.1.7 At 5.0 P.M.	2 Coys.entrain BIRR X Rds. 7.30 P.M. 2 " " " " " 10.00 P.M. Arrive VANCOUVER 8.30 P.M. and 11.0 P.M.respectively. Light Railway.
2/6th. Manc.Regt.	LIFE (Left)	2/9th. Manch.Regt.	HALIFAX E.14.c.2.5	2/4th. E/Lancsh.	Junc. CAMBRIDGE Rd.and ZONNEBEKE RD. I.5.a.25/70 At 5.0 P.M.	2 Coys.entrain BIRR X Rds. 7.30 P.M. 2 " " " " " 10.00 P.M. Arrive as above. Light Railway.
2/5th. Manch.Regt.	SUPPORT	2/10th. Manch.Regt.	CANAL AREA.	2/9th. Manch.Regt.	Junc.of MULE TRACK and CAMBRIDGE ROAD, I.11.b.1.7. At 11.30 a.m.	Move(after work) by Light Railway. Entrain at BIRR X Rds. 6.00 P.M. Detrain at MOAT FARM 5.00 P.M.
2/8th. Manch.Regt.	RESERVE	2/4th. E.Lancs.Regt.	INFANTRY BARRACKS, YPRES.	2/5th. E.Lancs.R.	As arranged by C.Os.	Move (after work) by Road.
199th. L.T.M.B.	LIFE	198th. L.T.M.B.	H.19.b.6.3	198th. L.T.M.B.	Junc. of MULE TRACK and CAMBRIDGE ROAD. I.11.b.1.7 At 11 a.m.	Move by Light Railway from BIRR X Rds. at 7.30 P.M.
199th. B.H.Q.	RAILWAY HOUSE	198th. Inf.Bde.	H.19.b.2.5	198th. B.H.Q.		Entrain BIRR X Roads at 7-30 P.M.

NOTES. Units proceeding by same train will entrain in order as above from front to rear. Entraining point will be reconnoitred beforehand. Units will appoint an entraining Officer who will meet a Brigade Staff Officer at BIRR KROSS ROADS at 7.0 P.M.

SECRET.   Copy No....

199th Infantry Brigade.

ADMINISTRATIVE ORDER

No. 58

Ref. MAP Sheet 28. 1/40,000

1. The 199th Inf. Bde. (Less M.G.Coy.) will relieve the 197th Inf. Bde., in the line January 28th and night of January 28th/29th.

2. All Transport lines and Q.M.Stores with the exception of those of Brigade H.Q. and 199th Brigade L.T.M.B. will stand fast.

3. BILLETING.
   2/5th Manch R. and L.T.M.B. will be Billeted at HUSSAR CAMP I.4.d.6.6 - these units will detail a billeting Party to reconnoitre the area on the 27th and arrange for necessary guides to conduct their Units to their billets on 28th.

4. BAGGAGE WAGONS Will report as under at 8.0 a.m. on 28th

Unit	No.	Location
Bde. H.Q.	1	H.19.b.2.5
2/5th Man.R.	2	H.18.c.3.1
2/6th " "	2	HALIFAX CAMP H.14.c.3.5
2/7th " "	2	VANCOUVER CAMP H.14.b.8.7
2/8th " "	2	INF. BARRACKS YPRES I.7.d.8.1
L.T.M.B.	1	VANCOUVER CAMP H.14.c.3.5

   Units will detail guides to await arrival of wagons.

5. AREA AND TRENCH STORES.
   Lists of all stores taken over will be forwarded to the Staff Captain. In addition separate receipts will be forwarded for reserve rations taken over.
   Officers commanding Battalions will arrange to detail one Officer to inspect personally reserve rations taken over in the Sector before signing receipts and will forward copies of receipts together with a certificate that they have been inspected to these H.Q. by 6.0 p.m. 29th.

6. Solidified Alchhol will be drawn by the two Battalions in the front line and 204th M.G.Coy from Bde. Q.M.S.

7. Trench Foot. Attention is called to 66th Division letter No. 2431/A dated 13.12.17.

8. Socks. Arrangements as A.O. No. 54.

9. Supplies. The train will deliver rations to the Q.M. Stores of the 2/5th and 2/8th Manch.R.

10. Runners. will be detailed as under and will report to the Staff Captain Infantry Barracks YPRES at 2.0 p.m. on 28th inst. and will be attached to B.H.Q. whilst Brigade is in the line.

Unit	No.
199th B.H.Q.	2
2/5th Man.R.	2
2/6th " "	2
2/7th " "	2
2/8th " "	2
204th M.G.Coy.	1
L.T.M.B.	1

(2).

11. **AMMUNITION.**
This can be drawn on demand from the Bomb Stores Gasometer ZONNEBEKE D.22.c.4.1.

12. **R.E. MATERIAL.**
Can be drawn from MOULIN FARM DUMP D.22.d.3.4.

13. **GUM BOOTS.**
The Brigade Gum Boot store is in Infantry Barracks YPRES, stock approximately 800 pairs. Wet Gum Boots in the line will be taken out by outgoing Units and must not be taken over. Units requiring Gum Boots can draw them from Brigade Gum Boot stores Infantry Barracks YPRES on the way up on 26th inst.
The procedure for the exchange of Gum Boots is as follows, wet Gum Boots are sent down in the Transports from the line and dry Gum Boots drawn in exchange from Infantry Barracks. Wet Gum Boots are dried under Divisional arrangements.

14. R.A.P's will provide hot drinks for any cases they may receive C.O's will indent for Beatrice Stoves for these posts if none are available.

15. **RETURNS.**
All administrative matters and returns will be dealt with at rear Brigade H.Q. Infantry Barracks YPRES from 2.0 p.m. 26th inst.

16. ACKNOWLEDGE.

J.S. Fox
Captain,
Staff Captain,
199th Infantry Brigade.

26.1.18.

Distribution.
Copy No.		
" " 1	....	G.O.C.
" " 2	....	Brigade Major.
" " 3	....	Staff Captain.
" " 4	....	Brigade Signal Officer.
" " 5	....	2/5th Manch R.
" " 6	....	2/6th " "
" " 7	....	2/7th " "
" " 8	....	2/8th " "
" " 9	....	204th M.G.Coy.
" " 10	....	199th L.T.M.B.
" " 11	....	544 Coy A.S.C.
" " 12	....	2/3rd Fld Amb.
" " 13	....	Q.M. 2/5th Manch R.
" " 14	....	" 2/6th " "
" " 15	....	" 2/7th " "
" " 16	....	" 2/8th " "
" " 17	....	66th Divl Train.
" " 18	....	66th Division "G"
" " 19	....	" " "A"
" " 20	....	War Diary
" " 21	....	" "
" " 22	....	File
" " 23	....	Spare.
" " 24	....	"

SECRET.   Copy No. 10

199th Infantry Brigade.
OPERATION ORDER NO 78.

Ref:- MAP Sheet 28. 1/40,000
            28. N.W.1 ZONNEBEKE 1/10,000

1. The 199th Inf. Bde.(less M.G.Coy) will relieve the 197th Inf. Bde. in the line on January 28th and night of January 28th/29th.

2. Reliefs will take place in accordance with attached table A.

3. (a) Working parties will be taken over in accordance with table B (1).

   (b) Working parties on January 28th will be found in accordance with Table B (11) attached.

4. All defence schemes, trench maps, trench stores, details of work in progress and proposed etc., will be taken over and receipts will be given for documents and stores.

5. Tracks are allotted as follows :-
   (a) Right Battalion and Support Battalion. "F" Track, Corduroy Road and ZONNEBEKE TRACK.
   (b) Left Battalion. IULT TRACK (alongside Railway from DEVIL'S CROSSING) and "K" Track.
   If tracks are being heavily shelled it is left to the discretion of C.O's to use tracks other than those allotted specially to them.

6. All other details of relief, guides etc., to be arranged between C.O's concerned.

7. Completion of relief will be reported to Brigade H.Q. by code sentence "ONE TORCH REQUIRED".

8. Command will pass on completion of relief.

9. ACKNOWLEDGE.

                                                   Captain.
                                                   Brigade Major.
26.1.18.   199th Infantry Brigade.

Distribution :-
  Copy No. 1 .... G.O.C.
            2 .... Brigade Major.
            3 .... Staff Captain.
            4 .... Bde.Signal Officer.
            5 .... 2/5th Manch Regt.
            6 .... 2/6th   "   "
            7 .... 2/7th   "   "
            8 .... 2/8th   "   "
            9 .... 204th M.G.Coy.
           10 .... 199th L.T.M.B.
           11 .... 197th Inf. Bde.
           12 .... 198th   "   "
           13 .... 66th Division "G"
           14 ....   "   "   "A"
           15 .... War Diary
           16 .... "   "
           17 .... File
           18 .... Spare.
           19 ....   "

TABLE A to accompany 199th Infantry Brigade Order No. 78.

Unit.	From	To.	Relieve	Route	Remarks.
199th Bde H.Q.	WINNIPEG CAMP	British H.Q. (D.28.a.5.5)	197th Bde H.Q.	YPRES - ZONNEBEKE RD	March route, arriving about 2.0 p.m.
2/5th Manch R.	CALAIS AREA	Line R.	2/7th Lan. Fus.	see para 5 (a)	March route, times to be arranged between C.O's but to be completed as soon after dark as possible.
2/6th Manch R.	HALIFAX CAMP.	Reserve. HUSSAR CAMP.	2/8th Lan. Fus.		Entrain VANCOUVER at 9.00 a.m. Detrain VLAMEY (POTIJZE) at 10.50 a.m.
2/7th Manch R.	VANCOUVER CAMP	SUPPORT (H.Q. Garter Pts.)	2/5th Lan. Fus.	see para 5 (a).	as for 2/5th Manch R.
2/8th Manch R.	INF. BARRACKS YPRES.	LINE (Left)	2/6th Lan. Fus.	see para 5 (b).	March route. Times to be arranged by C.O's but to be completed as soon after dark as possible.
199th L.T.M.B.	HALIFAX CAMP.	LINE	197th L.T.M.B.	YPRES-ZONNEBEKE RD.	By same train as 2/5th and 2/7th Manch Regts.

NOTE. Units will entrain in same order from the front of the train, 2/5th Man.R. 2/7th Man.R. 199th L.T.M.B. Units will be formed up ready to entrain punctually at the above time.

TABLE B (11) to accompany 199th Inf. Bde Order No. 78.

Parties to be found on January 28th 1918.

(vide table issued under this office No. G.71S d. 25.1.18).

SERIAL NO.	Whether found	REMARKS
1.	Yes.	This party will be found on the 28th and 29th Jan. by the 2/7th Man.R. The party will rejoin the 2/7th Man.R. as soon as possible on completion of work on the 29th.
2.(a)	No.	To be found by 2/6th Man.R. for Jan. 28th only.
2.(b)	Yes.	Details to be obtained from O.C. 2/7th Man.R. before leaving Camp on Jan. 28th. Work to start at 11.0 a.m.
3.	No.	
4.	No.	
5.(a)	Yes.	By 2/8th Manchester Regt.
5.(b)	No.	Will be found at 6.0 p.m. on Jan. 28th by 197th Inf. Bde.
6.	No.	

NOTE.- All parties on January 30th. are being found.

TABLE B (1) to accompany 199th Inf. Bde. order No. 78.

Serial No.	Unit.	Strength.	Working under supervision of.	Nature of Work.	Arrangements for rendezvous.	Unit not finding.	Remarks.
1.	2/5th Lan.R.	80	Field Coy.R.E.	Track maintenance	As arranged by R.E. Coy.	2/8th Lan.Fus.	Entrain ROUEN at 6.30 a.m. & move to GREY RUIN by Light Ry. thence to work by RD. Return.Entrain GREY RUIN at 1.0 p.m.
2.	"	50	"	Support line posts	"	"	
3.	"	75	"	Res. line posts.	"	"	
4.	"	50	"	ZONNEBEKE RD	"	"	
5.	"	two parties (a) & (b) of 25 men each.	1st Australian Tunnelling Coy.	Removing spoil bags	As arranged by Tun. Coy.	"	Party for ZONNEBEKE CH. can proceed by the Light Ry. as for Nos 1-4.

NOTE. 2/2 th Manchester Regt will obtain details of work from 2/8th Lan. Fus.

P.T.O.

Casualty Returns

CASUALTY RETURN.

UNIT "COD".

29.1.18. Lieut. J. S. Mayer, killed in action.
(2/8th Batt. Man. Regt. T.F.).

S. Egerton Lieut
for OC
COD

IV

Short Summary of events.

Army Form C. 2118.

WAR DIARY or INTELLIGENCE SUMMARY.
(Erase heading not required.)

Place	Date	Hour	Summary of Events and Information	Remarks and references to Appendices
	1918 Jan 31		From the 1st Jan to the 10th Jan 1918, the L.T.M.B. was in rest in the CAESTRE AREA — the time being employed in training. On the 11th Jan the Battery moved up to POTIJZE, and on the 12th Jan relieved the 146th L.T.M.B. in the BROODSEINDE RIDGE SECTOR. The Battery remained in this sector till the 22nd Jan, during which time guns were active against low-flying E.A. that crossed our lines. On the 22nd Jan the Battery was relieved by the 198th L.T.M.B. and went back to HALIFAX CAMP. The Battery remained in HALIFAX CAMP till the 27th Jan, and on the 28th Jan relieved the 197th L.T.M.B. in the L & R Ditch Sector in the line. On the 29th Jan LT. J.S. MAYER was killed by an enemy shell near Bty H.Q. DARING CROSSING. This Officer was buried at the MENIN RD. CEMETERY on the 31st Jan 1918. Up to the 31st Jan the guns were inactive in the left out-sector.	

William Marker Capt
O.C. 199th L.T.M.R.A.

(6339) Wt. W160/M3016 1,500,000 10/17 McA & W Ltd (E 1898) Forms W3091. Army Form W.3091.

Cover for Documents.

Nature of Enclosures.

CONFIDENTIAL

WAR DIARY

OF

199th L.T.M. BATTERY

FROM

1st FEB - 28th FEB.

VOLUME VII

Notes, or Letters written.

APPENDIX

I. OPERATION ORDERS

II. SHORT SUMMARY OF EVENTS for MONTH

III. T.P.R's

~~IV. CASUALTY RETURN~~

WAR DIARY
or
INTELLIGENCE SUMMARY.

(Erase heading not required.)

Army Form C. 2118.

Place	Date	Hour	Summary of Events and Information	Remarks and references to Appendices
LEFT ZONNEBEKE SECTOR	1/1/18		Smith river. Received B.O.O. no 79 copy no 10. Inter Section relief carried out. Commencing @ 3p.m. under cover of fog. Relief complete 4.15 p.m. S.S.L.	B.O.O. no 79 T.P.R 31/1/18 1/2/18
"	2		Smith river. S.S.L.	T.P.R. 1/2/18 2/2/18
"	3		Smith river. S.S.L.	T.P.R. 2/2/18 3/2/18
"	4		Smith river. S.S.L.	T.P.R. 3/2/18 4/2/18
"	5		Smith river. Received B.O.O. no 80 copy no 10. S.S.L. Inter section relief carried out without casualty. Commencing 6 p.m. Complete 7 p.m.	B.O.O. no 80 T.P.R. 4/2/18 5/2/18
"	6		Smith river. Received B.O.O. no 81 copy no 10. S.S.L. O.T.	B.O.O. no 81 T.P.R. 5/2/18 6/2/18

Army Form C. 2118.

WAR DIARY
or
INTELLIGENCE SUMMARY.
(Erase heading not required.)

Instructions regarding War Diaries and Intelligence Summaries are contained in F. S. Regs., Part II. and the Staff Manual respectively. Title pages will be prepared in manuscript.

Place	Date	Hour	Summary of Events and Information	Remarks and references to Appendices
LEFT ZONNEBEKE SECTOR	1918 Oct 7th		In Rulers &c.	TPR 6/9/18 7/9/18
"	" 8th		South line. Received amendment to B.O.O. no. 80 also 9635 O.B.5149 + 151 L.T.M.B. visited O. in H.Q. in the morning. &c.	amendment to BOO No 80 also 9635 7/9/18 8/9/18
"	" 9th		South line. This Battery was relieved in the line by the 149th L.T.M.B. (4 gun north half) & by the 151st L.T.M.B. (2 gun on the S. half) Relief commenced @ 3-15 and was completed by 4-45 p.m. The Section marched down to the R.O.D.D.IV. AREA HUSSAR CAMP. G.T.	
HUSSAR CAMP	" 10th		The Battery moved in accordance with B.O.O. no. 80. Complete Q.H.A. LIEAX. CAMP @ 6 p.m. G.T.	

Army Form C. 2118.

WAR DIARY
or
INTELLIGENCE SUMMARY.
(Erase heading not required.)

Instructions regarding War Diaries and Intelligence Summaries are contained in F. S. Regs., Part II. and the Staff Manual respectively. Title pages will be prepared in manuscript.

Place	Date	Hour	Summary of Events and Information	Remarks and references to Appendices
HALLIFAX CAMP.	1918 11-		The Battery made in accordance with B.O.O. No 80. Breaking camp. They were inspected by the G.O.C. on enroute. The Battery arrived @ School - Camp @ about midday. 2.64	
SCHOOL CAMP	12-		Training. Weather fine. 2.64	Brig Batt. to A. 899.
"	13		Training Weather wet. Received Brig Batt to A. 899 2.64	Brig Batt. to A. 899.
"	14		Training Weather fine. Received Brig Batt to A. 899 2.64	Brig Batt. to A. 440
"	15		Training Received Brig Batt of 648 also Zinfud G.T	

Army Form C. 2118.

WAR DIARY
or
INTELLIGENCE SUMMARY.
(Erase heading not required.)

Instructions regarding War Diaries and Intelligence Summaries are contained in F. S. Regs., Part II. and the Staff Manual respectively. Title pages will be prepared in manuscript.

Place	Date	Hour	Summary of Events and Information	Remarks and references to Appendices
SCHOOL CAMP	1918 Feb. 16th		Training and preparation for move. Weather fine.	
	17th		Moved out of camp at 5-15 a.m. and marched to PROVE IV STATION where the Battery entrained, booking @ 9 A.M. The Battery arrived at GUILLACOURT STATION @ 11-30 PM from where they marched in to BILLETS @ VAUVILLERS. See	
VAUVILLERS	18th		Weather fine. Training. See	
"	19th		Weather fine. Training.	A.W.O.L 16.2.18
"	20th		Weather fine. Training. A.T. 17.2.18 in Brigade Warning order. A.T. 20.2.18	B.W.O. 20.2.18
"	21st		Weather fine. Lt. Godsall concealed to hospital at	A.T.

D. D. & L., London, E.C. (A8604) Wt. W1771/M231 750,000 5/17 Sch. 52 Forms/C2118/14

Army Form C. 2118.

WAR DIARY
or
INTELLIGENCE SUMMARY.
(Erase heading not required.)

Instructions regarding War Diaries and Intelligence Summaries are contained in F. S. Regs., Part II. and the Staff Manual respectively. Title pages will be prepared in manuscript.

Place	Date	Hour	Summary of Events and Information	Remarks and references to Appendices
VAUVILLERS	22nd		Weather fine. Training. Received Brigade order No 81.	B.O.O No 81 Hy
—	23rd		Weather fine. Training. Received Amendment 15 B.O.O 81 Hy	Amdts to B.O.O 81 Hy
VILLERS CARBONNEL	24/9		Walter fine. Marched from VAUVILLERS to VILLERS-CARBONNEL. Ensuing at staging camp W. VILLERS-CARBONNEL about 1.15 p.m. Received B.O.O.82.	B.O.O. 82 Admin O. 38 a.T.
URAIGNES	25/9		Weather wet. Left staging camp at 10.A.M. & marched to billets at URAIGNES. arriving about 2.30 p.m. Received Brigade memo. A981. a.T.	B/g19: Memo. A.981.
R.Sub-nd/26th VILLERS sect.	26/9		Weather fine. Marched from URAIGNES at 10.A.M. & lined 2nd & 7 M B in the line, relief completed without casualties at 3.30 p.m. a.T.	T.P.R 28/2/18.
—	27th		Weather unsettled. In the line a.T.	T.P.R 29/2/18.
—	28th		Weather unsettled. In the line a.T.	

Operation Opdsps.

SECRET.
199th Infantry Brigade
OPERATION ORDER NO 79.

Copy No....

Ref :- MAP Sheet 28 N.E.1 1/10,000
      "   28 1/40,000

1. On the night of Feb. 3/4th, the following reliefs will take place.
   (a) 2/5 Manch Regt. from Right Front Line to Reserve in HUSSAR Camp.
   (b) 2/8   "   "   "   Left   "   "   "   SUPPORT.
   (c) 2/6   "   "   "   Reserve   to Right Front Line
   (d) 2/7   "   "   "   Support   to Left Front Line.

2. Relief to be completed as soon after dark as possible.

3. Command of Battalion subsectors to pass on completion of relief.

4. (a) O.C. 2/6th Man. Regt. and O.C. 2/7th Man. Regt., will follow the organisation and method of work as carried out by O.C. 2/5th Man. Regt., and O.C. 2/8th Man. Regt., namely in accordance with 66th Division 685/12 G of 22.1.18.
   (b) All details of work in progress and proposed will be taken over.
   (c) A new table of working parties to be found by Support and Reserve Battalions is being issued separately ; details of any small parties not included on this table will also be handed over.
   (d) The two forward companies of the Support Battalion are at the entire disposal of C.O's Front Line Battalions, one company apiece for working purposes.

5. All defence schemes, trench maps, trench stores etc., will be handed over and receipts obtained.

6. 2/7th Man. Regt., will be clear of the line ZONNEBEKE X Roads - ZONNEBEKE STA., by 5.0 p.m.: 2/6th Man. Regt., will not reach this line till 5.15 p.m.. For withdrawal 2/5th Man. Regt., should use Corduroy Road N. of the railway line from SPINE, 2/8th Man. Regt., will use ZONNEBEKE TRACK. In case of heavy shelling routes may be altered at C.O's discretion.

7. All other details of relief to be arranged by C.O's.

8. Completion of relief to be reported to this office by code number 34.

9. ACKNOWLEDGE.

                                           J.S.Fox
                                           Captain.
                                           Brigade Major.
1st. Feb., 1918.   199th Infantry Brigade.

Distribution :-
   Copy No. 1......... G.O.C.   Distribution (contd)
             2......... Brigade Major.   Copy No.16 ... 66th Div.G
             3......... Staff Captain.   17 ...   A
             4......... Bde. Signal Officer.   18 ... War Diary
             5......... 2/5th Manch Regt.   19 ...   "
             6......... 2/6th "   "   20 ... File.
             7......... 2/7th "   "   21 ... Spare
             8......... 2/8th "   "   22 ...   "
             9......... 204th M.G.Coy
            10......... 199th L.T.M.B.
            11......... 202nd M.G.Coy.
            12......... 203rd   "
            13......... 198th Inf. Bde.
            14......... 150th Inf. Bde.
            15......... C.R.E. 66th Div.

SECRET.   Copy No. 10

199th Infantry Brigade.
OPERATION ORDER NO 80

Ref:- MAP Sheet 27 & 28. 1/40,000
              28NE 1/10,000.

Withdrawal of 199th Inf.Bde   1. The 199th Infantry Brigade will be withdrawn from the line on the night of Feb. 9/10th. On Feb 10th the Brigade will concentrate in the RENINGHELST area and on Feb 11th will move to the Divisional Concentration area.

Transfer of Front.   2. (a) On the night of Feb 7/8 the 199th Infantry Brigade will take over that portion of the front at present held by the 197th Infantry Brigade between the present inter-Brigade boundary and point D.23.d.1.7. This includes support Post No. 9 and Front Line Posts D.23. 10 to D.23. 16 inclusive.
(b) O.C. 2/6th Manchester Regt will arrange all details of this transfer direct with O.C. 2/8th Lancs. Fusiliers.
(c) Command will pass on completion of relief.
(d) Completion will be reported by code number 48.

Relief.   3. (a) On the night of Feb. 9/10 the following reliefs will take place.
2/8th Manch. Regt. will be relieved in Right Front Line by the 4th Northumberland Fusiliers, 149th Inf.Bde.
2/7th Manch Regt. will be relieved in Left Front Line by the 5th Border Regt. 151st Inf. Bde.
(b) All Reliefs will be carried out in accordance with attached Table A., and battalions will be accommodated that night as shown in the Table.

Details of Relief.   4. (a) Details of relief 2/6th Manch. Regt and 2/7th Manch. Regt. will be arranged between C.O's concerned. H.Q. of 4th N.F. and 5th Border Regt., will be at SEINE and HAMBURG respectively, previous to Feb. 9th.
(b) Lists of Position calls and any Secret documents, maps and aeroplane photographs etc., which will be of use to the incoming battalions will be handed over on relief and receipts taken. All other old schemes, maps and papers will be burnt. A copy of receipt will be forwarded to Brigade H.Q. on Feb.10th, together with copies of receipts for trench stores handed over. The 2/8th Manch Regt will send over to 5th Northumberland Fus. at SEINE any maps of the sector track maps etc., that are likely to be of use, and will burn all other correspondence. The 2/5th Manch Regt will hand over maps to 5th Northumberland Fus. at WHITE FARM CAMP POTIJZE in a similar manner.
(c) Completion of relief to be notified by code number "25".
(d) H.Q. 149th Inf. Bde. will take over V.R. dugout from 199th Inf. Bde. and G.O.C. 199th Inf. Bde. will relinquish command on completion of relief.

Reconnaissance   5. (a) On the evening of Feb 8th, 5th Border Regt. is sending 1 Officer per company and 1 N.C.O. and 1 guide per platoon to take over details of Line held by 2/7th Manch Regt. The guides detailed will be taken over the route by guides of their opposite numbers and will, together with those guides, guide in their own units on the night of Feb 9/10.

P.T.O.

2.

5. (b) Officers and N.C.O's of 4th M.F. will be given every opportunity of seeing the 2/8 Man. area before taking over.
    (c) A copy of patrol reports since battalions have been in the line will be handed over to relieving Battalion.

Work. 6. Working parties detailed in Table issued under this office number B.M./89/6 of 1.2.18 will cease to be found on Feb. 9th.

M.G.Coy 7. Details of relief of 294th Machine Gun Coy. are being arranged by D.M.G.O. On relief the 294th Machine Gun Coy., will withdraw to transport lines, whence it will move under orders of this Brigade.

Moves. 8. (a) On Feb 10th Brigade H.Q., 2/5th Manch. Regt and 2/7th Manch Regt will move to HALIFAX area in accordance with Table B (to be issued later)
    (b) On Feb 11th the 199th Infantry Brigade group (including 432nd Fd. Coy and 2/3rd Fd. Amb.) will move to SCHOOL CAMP L3.d. (Sheet 27) in accordance with Table C (to be issued later.).

Signal Schools. 9. (a) All students at the Brigade Signal School will rejoin units on Feb. 10th in REFINGHELST and HALIFAX Camp areas.
    (b) All students at the Divisional signal school will rejoin their units on Feb. 11th.

Brigade H.Q. 10. (a) On relief on the night of Feb. 9/10th, Bde H.Q. will close at V.R.dugout and move to GORDON Area reopening on arrival.
    (b) On Feb. 10th Bde H.Q. will close at Gordon area at 10.0 a.m. and reopen in HALIFAX area on arrival.
    (c) On Feb. 11th Bde H.Q. will close at HALIFAX area at 9.0 a.m. and reopen at SCHOOL CAMP on arrival.

11. ACKNOWLEDGE.

J.S. Fox Captain.
For Brigade Major.
199th Infantry Brigade.

5.2.18.

Distribution :-
```
Copy No.  1 ........ G.O.C.
          2 ........ Brigade Major.
          3 ........ Staff Captain.
          4 ........ Bde. Signal Officer.
          5 ........ 2/5th Manch Regt.
          6 ........ 2/3th    "     "
          7 ........ 2/7th    "     "
          8 ........ 2/8th    "     "
          9 ........ 304th M.G.C.
         10 ........ 199th L.T.M.B.
         11 ........ 197th Inf. Bde.
         12 ........ 149th   :   :
         13 ........ 151st   :   :
         14 ........ 66th Division "G"
         15 ........   "      "    "A"
         16 ........ 432nd Fd. Coy R.E.
         17 ........ 544th Coy A.S.C.
         18 ........ 66th Div. C.R.E.
         19 ........ War Diary.
         20 ........   "    "
         21 ........ File
         22 ........ Spare
         23 ........   "
         24 ........ 2/3rd Field Ambulance.
```

SECRET.   Copy No. 10

                     199th Infantry Brigade
                     ADMINISTRATIVE ORDER
                            No. 37.

            Ref MAP Sheet 27 - 18.

            Administrative instructions issued with reference to
            199th Infantry Brigade Operation Order No. 80.

Billets.   (a) Units will be billeted in accordance with attached
                Table A.

Billeting   (b) To report on the day before move takes place to Area
Parties.   Commandants POTIJZE, GORDON, REININGHELST, HALIFAX and
                CANAL Area's.

            (c) Rear parties (including an officer) will in all cases
                be left behind to clean up camps and transport lines, and
                a signed statement will invariably be obtained from Area
                Commandants concerned to the effect that the camp has been
                left in a satisfactory condition.
                    Particular attention is to be paid to the incineration of
                all refuse.

            (d) Details left out of trenches will rejoin their units on
                the 10th.

            (e) Billeting Parties consisting of 1 officer 1 O.R. and
                3 cyclists per unit for the School Camp L.3.d. will report
                to A/Staff Captain at 8 a.m. on the 10th at Reserve Brigade
                H.Q., H.19.b.2.3 WINNIPEG CAMP. Rations will be carried
                for 11th.

                                        Reserve Bde.H.Q. H.19.b.2.3
Lorries.   Lorries for conveyance of Baggage will report at 8.0 a.m.
            on the 11th. Lorries will do two journeys if required.
            Guides for lorries will report at Staff Captains office
            at 7.45 a.m. Lorries will be allotted as under :-
                        B.H.Q.   1
                        2/5th Man. R.   1
                        2/6th Man. R.   1
                        2/7th Man. R.   1
                        2/8th Man. R.   1
                        204th M.G.C.   1
                        199th L.T.M.B.   1

                An officer will in all cases be detailed to take charge
            of convoys of Lorries or single lorries.

Supplies
Arrangements during move will be as under.
                                                 For
   Date.   Units.   Refills.   Consumption   Remarks.

 Feb 8th   199th Inf.Bde.   1 p.m.   10th   as at present
  " 9th   -do-   After arrival   11th   Supplies to be
                              of supplies   delivered to
                              from R.Head.   units by Train
                                                           Transport.
  " 9th   2/3rd Fd.Amb.   1 p.m.   11th   as at present.
  " 10th   199th Inf.Bde.   After arrival   12th   By Train Trans-
                              of supplies   port & delivered
                              from R.Head.   to units at
                                                           SCHOOL CAMP on
                                                           11th.

                                                            P. T. O.

Date.	Units.	Refills.	For Consumption	Remarks.
Feb 10th	432nd Fd.Coy.	7.30 a.m.	11th	as at present.
Feb 10th	-do-	After arrival of supplies from R.Head.	12th	By train Coy to School Camp on the 11th.
" 11th	2/3rd Fd.Amb.	10.0 a.m.	12th	Drawn from Refilling point School Camp by units own transport & daily thereafter.
" 11th	199th Inf.Bde.	10.0 a.m.	13th	By units own transport & daily thereafter.
" 12	432nd Fd.Coy.	10.0 a.m.	13th	Drawn from refilling point by Units own Transport & daily thereafter.

Locations of Refilling point new area will be notified to Units later.

Baggage Wagons. Baggage wagons will report to Units transport lines on the evening before moving and will rejoin the respective Coys. of the Divisional Train as soon as possible after arrival in the new area.

Medical. The 2/3rd Field Ambulance will be at SCHOOL CAMP.

Ordnance. The DIVISIONAL ORDNANCE STORE will remain open at REININGHELST until the 9th instant inclusive, and will open at PROVEN on the 11th inst.

Div. Laundry & Baths. Personnel from Div. Baths and Laundry will be returned to their units on the 11th inst., under Div. arrangements.

Baths. Bathing arrangements in new area will be notified later.

Employed Men. All officers and men employed in present Divisional Area in accordance with this Brigade number A 615 of 7/1/18 will be returned to their units as under.

Serial No.	Duty.	Numbers employed Off O.R.	When & by whom to be relieved.	Disposal on relief.	Remarks.
1	Area Comd PIONEER	1 2/6	Not to be relieved	To rejoin Unit on 10th inst.	
2	Area Comd POTIJZE Area and Staff.	1 9 2/7	New Zealand Division. 9th.	To rejoin their Unit.	One lorry will report at 9 am on 10th inst to Area Comd. POTIJZE who will arrange to pick up personnel in serial No. 1 & further instructions sent direct to Lt. Hutchinson.
3	Helpers YMCA Hut.	12	Under arrangements of Supt. Y.M.C.A. Hut.	To report Bde HQ on 10th	

3.

Area and Trench Stores

(a) All Area and Trench Stores, Ammunition, Reserve Rations and Water will be handed over to relieving Units and area Commandants concerned and receipt obtained and copies forwarded to this office by 9 a.m. Feb 10th.

(b) Certificate that no Stores of any kind have been taken from the Corps Area except such Stores as are allowed by War Establishments or amending G.R.Os will be forwarded by O.C. units to reach these H.Q. by Feb. 11th. It should be noted that a certificate to the above effect has to be rendered to 22nd Corps by the G.O.C. on behalf of the Division.

Instructions for handing over Stores.

1. On relief the following stores will be brought out by units and will not be handed over:-
    All Tulor Picks & Turplines, if any.
    All waterproof ration bags.
    All anti-aircraft sights for Lewis and Machine Guns.
    All white patroling suits.
    All dummy S.A.A.
    Emergency Ammunition Carriers, according to the scale laid down in G.R.O. 2080.

2. All wagons and water carts will be complete with water tins. Units will report to this office by Feb 10th number of L.G.S. wagons not fitted for water tins and number of water tins required to complete.

3. Units will march out with their full establishment of S.A.A. Grenades and tools. The following should be in possession :-

	With Lewis Guns or Machine Guns.	Mobile Reserve.
S.A.A. Infantry Battalions	39088	78000
S.A.A. M.G.Coy.	128000	-
Grenades, Infantry Batt.		768

Tools

	Picks	Shovels
Infantry Bn	76	110
" Bde H.Q.	538	538
M.G.Coy	20	20

4. Particular care will be taken in handing over
    Soyer Stoves
    Beatrice "
    Anti-Aircraft Mountings.
    Foot troughs
    Gum Boots.
    Braziers.
    Hot Food Containers.
    Water tins.

5. All pack saddlery surplus to establishment laid down in mobilisation store table will be handed in to D.A.D.O.S. Store forthwith, and numbers handed in reported to these Headquarters by 1st D.R. Feb. 11th.

Gum Boots.

All wet Gum Boots will be handed in at Infantry Barracks YPRES. Dry ones will be handed over.

ACKNOWLEDGE.

J S Fox Captain.
Staff Captain.
199th Infantry Brigade.

6th Feb. 1918.

P.T.O.

Distribution.
```
Copy No.  1  ........  G.O.C.
  "   "   2  ........  Brigade Major
  "   "   3  ........  Staff Captain.
  "   "   4  ........  Brigade Signal Officer.
  "   "   5  ........  2/5th Manch R.
  "   "   6  ........  2/6th    "    "
  "   "   7  ........  2/7th    "    "
  "   "   8  ........  2/8th    "    "
  "   "   9  ........  304th M.G.Coy.
  "   "  10  ........  199th L.T.M.B.
  "   "  11  ........  544 Coy. A.S.C.
  "   "  12  ........  2/3rd Fd. Amb.
  "   "  13  ........  O.H. 2/5th Manch R.
  "   "  14  ........   "   2/6th   "   "
         15  ........   "   2/7th   "   "
         16  ........   "   2/8th   "   "
         17  ........  66th Divn Train.
         18  ........  66th Division G.
         19  ........         "        A.
         20  ........  Area Commandants POTIJZE
         21  ........         "       "   GORDON.
         22  ........         "       "   YPRES S Sub-Area.
         23  ........         "       "   CANAL.
         26  ........         "       "   PIONEER.
         27  ........         "       "   HALIFAX.
         28  ........         "       "   REININGHELST.
         29  ........         "       "   ST JANSTER-BIEZEN.
         30  ........  199th Bde Transport Officer.
         31  ........  War Diary.
         32  ........    "    "
         33  ........  File.
         34  ........  Spare.
         35  ........    "
         36  ........  149th Inf. Bde.
         37  ........  151st  "    "
```

TABLE "A"

Unit.	Night 9/10th Feb. Billets.	Transport. Q.M.Strs.	Night 10/11th Feb. Billets.	Transport. Q.M.S.	Night 11/12th Feb. Billets.	Transport.	Remarks.
B.H.Q.	I.8.d.5.7 Gordon Area Billets vacated by 421 F.Coy.	Stands fast.	WINNIPEG CAMP Reserve Bde H.Q. H.19.b.2.3	Stands fast	SCHOOL CAMP L 3 d Sheet 27	L 3 d	
2/5th Han.R.	RENINGHELST Area.	—do—	RENINGHELST Area	—do—	SCHOOL CAMP	—do—	
2/6 " "	HUSSAR LAST POTIJZE Area	—do—	HALIFAX CAMP HALIFAX Area	—do—	"	—do—	
2/7 " "	DRAGON CAMP POTIJZE Area	—do—	VANCOUVER CAMP HALIFAX Area.	—do—	"	—do—	
2/8th " "	RENINGHELST	—do—	REN/INGHELST Area	—do—	"	—do—	
304 M.G.Coy *	CANAL Area Present Billets				"	—do—	
199th L.T.M.B.	GORDON Area as Bde H.Q.		HALIFAX CAMP	—do—	"	—do—	
452nd Fd Coy	SAPPER CAMP	Stands fast	SAPPER CAMP	—do—	"	—do—	
2/3rd Fd Amb.	WARATAH CAMP	—do—	WARATAH CAMP	—do—	"	—do—	
744 Coy ASC	RENINGHELST	—do—	RENINGHELST	—do—	"	—do—	

* Night of 8/9th 304th M.G.Coy will be billeted at CANAL Area.

TABLE "A"

Date.	Unit.	From.	To.	Relieved by.	Remarks.
Feb.7/8	2/8th L.R.				Takes over line in accordance with para 2 (a) now held by 2/8th Lan. Fus.
" 8/10	2/5th N.R.	Right Front Line	HUSSAR CAMP	4th Northumberland Fusiliers.	4th N.F. will be at SWIPE for two or three days before the relief.
"	2/7th N.R.	Left Front Line	DRAGON CAMP	5th Border Regiment.	H.Q. of 5th Border R. at HAMBURG from Feb 8th will not change on relief 5th Border R. will not leave HAMBURG before 5.30 p.m.
" 9th	2/5th N.R.	Reserve.	RENINGHELST AREA.	6th Northumberland Fusiliers.	6th N.F. will be accommodated in "HUT" FARM CAMP. 2/5th March R. will move by Light Railway from POTIJZE to RENINGHELST (time notified later)
" 9th	2/8th N.R.	Support.	Reningholst Area.	No relief.	H.Q. and 2 Coys will move to POTIJZE without relief at 5.0 p.m. The 2 Coys in support to front line battalions will move as follows:— Coy. at THAMES at 5.15 p.m., Coy at DARING CROSSING at 5.30 p.m.
" 9/10	Bde H.Q. Line		GORDON Area.	149th Inf. Bde.	Personnel (except G.O.C. and Bde Major) will be relieved by 3.0 p.m. Command to pass on completion of relief.
"	199th L.T.M.B. Line		GORDON Area.	149th L.T.M.B.	Details and times of relief to be arranged between O.C's.

NOTE: (a) Units withdrawing from the line and forward areas must move in very small parties not larger than sections until west of FREZENBERG RIDGE.
(b) Tracks S. of Railway allotted to Right Battalion. N. of Railway to Left Battalion West of Devil's Crossing, both units may use ZONNEBEKE ROAD.

SECRET

Amendment to 199th Infantry Brigade.   Copy No... 10
Operation Order No. 80.

Reference 199th Infantry Brigade Order No. 80, the following amendments and addition will be made :-

(a) In para 4 b (last line) and Table "A" remarks column line 8, for "WHITE FARM CAMP" substitute "WHITBY CAMP".

(b) Table A. 2/5th Manchester Regt., Remarks column add "The battalion will concentrate at POTIJZE and move by Light Railway to NEWINGHURST AREA" (Time of entrainment will be notified later).

                                     Captain.
                               Brigade Major.
B.H.Q.   199th Infantry Brigade.
8th Feb, 1918.

TO all recipients of 199th Infantry Brigade Order No. 80.

TO :-
O.C.   O.C.

2/5th Manch Regt.   422nd Fd. Coy. R.E.
2/6th   "   "   544th Coy. A.S.C.
2/7th   "   "   2/3rd Field Amb.
2/8th   "   "   66th Division "Q") for
294th M.G.Coy.   66th Division "G") information.
199th L.T.M.B.

Reference 199th Infantry Brigade Order No. 80

1. On February 9th the 2/5th Manchester Regt., and 2/8th Manchester Regt., will move to RENINGHELST AREA by train as follows :-
   (a) 2/5th Manch. Regt., entrain VINERY I.5.b.6.5 at 3.0 p.m. detrain ROBSON G.28.a.9.1. Billet RENINGHELST G.22.a.2.4.
   (b) 2/8th Manch Regt., entrain VINERY 7.30 p.m., detrain ROBSON Billets as follows :-
       Bn. H.Q. and 60 O.R's   RENINGHELST.
       280 O.R's   G.34.a.0.4
       170   "   G.27.b.5.7

2. There will be no Table B. Brigade H.Q., 2/6th Manch Regt., 2/7th Manch Regt., and 199th L.T.M.B. will move to Halifax Area by train about 9.30 a.m. on February 10th. Details of trains will be issued later to all concerned.

3. Table C. will be issued later.

B.H.Q.
8th Feb. 1918.

Captain.
Brigade Major.
199th Infantry Brigade.

SECRET

TABLE "C" (to accompany 199th Infantry Brigade Order No. 80)

March Table for February 11th 1918.

Units in order of march	From	To.	Time at Bde starting point X roads G.9.d.5.1	Subsidiary Starting Point.	Time	Route.	Remarks.
Bde H.Q.	WINNIPEG CAMP.	School Camp L.3.d.(Sheet 27)	7.28 a.m.	Road Junc H.13.d.95.20	7.04 a.m.		
2/6th Man.R.	HALIFAX CAMP	-do-	7.32 a.m.	-do-	7.08 a.m.		
2/7th "	VANCOUVER CAMP	-do-	8.0 a.m.	-do-	7.26 a.m.		
2/5th "	G.22.a.2.4	-do-		G.4.d.5.4	8.38 a.m.	G.13.b.5.1 to } need not go by G.15.b - G4d } BRANDHOEK go G.27.d.8.6 to } by G.DB b-G4d. G.15b - G4d }	
-2/8th "	RENINGHELST	-do-		-do-	8.53 a.m.		
199th L.T.M.B.	HALIFAX CAMP	-do-	9.04 a.m.	H.13.d.95.20	8.30 a.m.		
204th M.G.C. plus 3 guns 202 M.G.C.	BELGIAN CHAT.	-do-	9.08 a.m.	H.13.d.2.2	8.09 a.m.	VLAMERTINGHE	
432nd Fd Co.	SAPPER CAMP Potijze.	-do-	9.15 a.m.			YPRES - VLA- MERTINGHE.	To proceed indep-
544th A.S.C.	RENINGHELST	-do-	9.25 a.m.	H.13.b.1.2	9.08 a.m.		endently and to arrive SCHOOL CAMP by 10th February 1.0 p.m.
2/3rd Fd Amb.	WARATAH CAMP	-do-				To proceed independently of Bde.	

NOTE.- 1 Strict march discipline must be observed.
2 The attention of all concerned is directed to Fourth Army No. G.S.149, issued under 66th Div. No. 527/2 G of 22.12.17, regarding distances to be kept on the march, and places where troops and transport may not be halted.

TO:—

O.C.
 2/5th Manchester Regt.
 2/6th " "
 2/7th " "
 2/8th " "
 204th Machine Gun Coy.

O.C.
 199th L.T.M.B.
 452nd Fd. Coy R.E.
 544th Coy A.S.C.
 2/3rd Fd. Ambulance.
 G.O.C.

 Reference Brigade Operation Order No. 80 :— The following points will be carefully observed.

1. Steel helmets will be worn and rifles slung over right shoulder.
2. Eyes right (or left) by Platoons. Officers saluting with right hand.
3. All Signallers will march in a formed body in front of Battalions.
4. Prescribed halts will be observed with the exception of the halt at 9.50 which will be for 15 minutes (9.50 a.m. to 10.5 a.m.) to allow for correction of any mistakes in intervals.
5. Bands will play on the march.
6. All transport vehicles must be washed this evening.
7. The following distances will be observed by <u>Brigade H.Qrs.</u> Between it and its Transport 100 yards, and between its transport and the head of the loading Battalion (2/6thM/C) 100 yards.
8. All sick and unfit men should be disposed of before marching tomorrow.
9. Special attention is called to distances between transport – see Fourth Army No. G.S. 148.
10. The order of march of Transport will be as follows:—

   10 Limbers.
   2 Water Carts.
   4 Trav. Kitchens.
   1 Maltose Cart.
   1 Officer's Mess Cart.
   2 Baggage Wagons.

B.H.Q.
10th Feb. 1918.

       Captain.
       A/Brigade Major.
       199th Infantry Brigade.

SECRET.

O.C.	O.C.
2/5th Manchester Regt.	199th L.T.M.B.
2/6th " "	452nd Fd. Coy R.E.
2/7th " "	2/3rd Fd. Ambulance.
2/8th " "	544th Coy A.S.C.
204th Machine Gun Coy.	

In continuation of this office A 899 of 12.2.18.

1. Advanced parties will have guides at GUILLAUCOURT STATION to meet units 9 hours after the scheduled time of departure from PROVEN.

2. Following table shows times at which units entrain.

Entraining Station - PROVEN
Detraining Station - GUILLAUCOURT.

Serial No.	Date.	No. of March	Time of Starting (hours)	UNITS.
1	17th	HT57	4.00	H.Q. Pioneer Bn. and 3 Companies & transport of Pioneer Bn. and 1 Coy. cooker & team of 2/5th Man. Rgt.
2	17th	HT60	7.00	2/5th Man. Rgt. (less 1 Coy. cooker & team).
3	17th	HT63	10.00	199 Bde HQ. Bde.Signal Section. Bde.M.G.Coy. Bde.T.M.B. 1 Coy. cooker & team of 2/6th Man.Rgt.
4	17th	HT66	13.00	2/6th Man.Rgt. less 1 Coy. cooker & team.
5	17th	HT72	19.00	452 Field Coy. 544 Coy A.S.C.
6	17th	HT81	22.00	2/3rd E.L.Fld.Amb. Div. Salvage Coy. Div.Laundry personnel. Div.Band.Div.Concert Party.
7	18th	HT54	1.00	2/7th Man.Rgt. (less 1 Coy. cooker & team).
8	18th	HT57	4.00	2/8th Man.Rgt.Transport and 1 Coy.cooker & team of 2/7th Man.Rgt. Mobile Vet.Section. D.A.D.O.S. Stores.

3. 199th Infantry Brigade H.Q. and whole group will be billeted at VILLERS-BRETONNEUX scheduled accommodation :-

Offrs.	Other Ranks.	Horses.
200	4,000	450.

Area Commandant :- COL. CHILDERS, 34 BIS RUE D'AMIENS,
VILLERS BRETONNEUX,
(5th Army Administrative Area Commandant).

J.S. Fox
Captain.
Staff Captain.
199th Infantry Brigade.

B.H.Q.
13th Feb. 1918.

SECRET.

66th Divn.
3902/7/Q.

O.C.,
2/5th Manchester Regt.
2/6th   "   "
2/7th   "   "
204th Machine Gun Coy.
199th L.T.M.B.
2/3rd Fd. Ambulance.
432nd Field Co. R.E.

O.C.,
544th Coy A.S.C.
O.C. 2/5th Manch. Regt.
   "   2/6th   "
   "   2/7th   "
199th Bde. Transport Officer.
2/8th Man.R. Transport Officer.

MOVE TO FIFTH ARMY AREA.

Moves by Rail. 1. Units will proceed by rail in accordance with table issued under this office A.899 of 15.2.18.
Entraining station for all units will be PROVEN.
Detraining   "   "   "   "   "   GUILLAUCOURT.
(15 miles E. of AMIENS)
Approximate length of journey 10 hours.
All trains halt 1 hour for refreshment at TINCQUES.

Instructions with regard to entrainment. 2. (a) All trains consist of 1 Officers' carriage, 17 flat trucks, 30 covered trucks.
Each flat truck will take an average of 4 axles.
Each covered truck will take 6 H.D. horses, or 8 L.D. horses or mules, or 40 men.
No personnel or stores will be allowed in the brake vans at each end of the train, or on the roofs of the trucks.
No covered trucks are to be used for baggage or stores without the permission of the DIVISIONAL STAFF OFFICER superintending the entrainment.
(b) Fatigue parties each of two officers and 100 other ranks will be detailed for loading duty at entraining and detraining stations as follows :-

Trains.	For Entraining	For Detraining	Remarks.
2 to 8 (this office A.899)	(a) 2 Officers & 100 men detailed by 199th Inf. Bde.	(b) 2 Officers & 100 men detailed by 199th Inf. Bde.	(a) To be included in Coy. 2/7th M.R. travelling on 8th train. (b) To be included in the 3 Coys. 2/5th M.R. on 2nd train.

NOTE:- 1. Entraining parties will report to the R.T.O. at the entraining station 3 hours before the departure of the first train they are loading.
2. The officer in charge of each detraining party will report to the R.T.O. immediately on arrival at the detraining station.

(c) All units other than Infantry Battalions will arrive complete at the entraining station 3 hours before the departure of the train.
Transport and all baggage of Infantry Battns will arrive at the entraining station 3 hours before the departure of the train, but the dismounted personnel will arrive 1½ hours later.

Continued........

- 2 -

Instructions with regard to entrainment.

2. (d) A complete marching out state showing numbers of men, horses, G.S., limbered G.S., two-wheeled carts, cycles and truck loads of surplus baggage will be sent to the R.T.O. with the transport of every unit so that accommodation on the train can be checked by the R.T.O. at the beginning of entrainment.
NOTE:- 1 truck load = 3 lorry loads.

(e) Supply and baggage wagons will accompany their units in every case.

(f) The entrainment of all units must be completed half an hour before the time of departure of the train.
Detraining station must be cleared of all baggage, transport and personnel 24 hours after arrival.

(g) Breast ropes for horse trucks must be provided by units themselves; ropes for lashing vehicles on flat trucks will be provided by the R.T.O.

(h) The senior officer on the train will be responsible for the discipline of the troops and will picquet both ends of the train at every stop to prevent troops leaving.

(k) All doors of covered trucks and carriages on the right hand side of the train, when on the main line, will be kept closed.

(l) Attention is called to S.S.544 "TRAINS MOVING WITH TROOPS" which has been circulated to Infantry Brigade Headquarters and DIVISIONAL ARTILLERY.

Billeting.

3. On arrival, the Division will occupy the PROYART Area.
Billets are allotted as shown in para 3 of this office A.899 of 13.2.18.

Lorries for Baggage.

4. Lorries for conveyance of baggage to the entraining station will be detailed in accordance with the attached Table "B".
Similar numbers of lorries will be detailed at the detraining station by the D.A.A.G., 39th Division, from the pool of lorries at his disposal.
Loading and unloading of lorries will be carried out as expeditiously as possible, and baggage must arrive at the entraining station 3 hours before departure of the train, and leave the detraining station 24 hours after arrival.
In the new area lorries transporting baggage from the detraining station will not dump at individual billets.
Baggage will be dumped at one central dump only in each village and the lorries will return immediately to GUILLAUCOURT.

Supplies.

5. The attached Table A shows the supply arrangements for all units during the period of the move.
Refilling points in the new area will be notified direct to units by the affiliated Train Company as soon as possible after arrival.

Continued......

- 3 -

Supplies.	5.	The S.S.O. or his representative will be found at GUILLAUCOURT Station from noon on the 15th inst. until the morning of 18th instant when Divisional Train Headquarters will be open at HARBONNIERS.
Ordnance.	6.	The Divisional Ordnance Store at PROVEN will close at 4.0 p.m. on the 16th instant and open at HARBONNIERS at 9.0 a.m. on the 19th instant.
Medical.	7.	Field Ambulances will be responsible for the collection and evacuation of sick from all units in their respective Groups from the time of arrival in the new area.
		As soon as possible after arrival in the new area the A.D.M.S. will arrange to open a Divisional Rest Station.
Post.	8.	The Divisional Mail will be delivered in the present area for the last time on the 17th instant and the postal lorries will proceed on that date to the new area with mails for units that depart on the 15th and 16th instant.
		The Divisional Mail will be delivered in the PROYART Area on and after the 17th instant, and mails for units moving on and after that date will be detained at the Divisional Post Office until their arrival.
Baths, etc.	9.	Arrangements with regard to Baths, Laundry, Canteens, Theatres, etc., in the PROYART Area will be notified later.
Leave.	10.	Until further orders all leave vacancies will be via BOULOGNE as at present, and the present allotments will remain in force.
		Units should arrange with the Area Commandants of their present areas to accommodate personnel proceeding on leave during the two days following the day of departure, and such officers or men will proceed from POPERINGHE by the present Leave Train.
		Care will be taken that men left behind in this manner are in possession of sufficient rations for their journey as well as of an advance of pay and the necessary certificates with regard to bathing etc.
		On arrival at GUILLAUCOURT Station Os.C. units will ascertain leave arrangements from the Divisional Staff Officer superintending detrainment.
		The Divisional Railhead Disbursing Officer will leave POPERINGHE on the morning of the 17th instant, and travel with Divisional Headquarters.
Area Stores.	11.	All Area and Billet stores in charge of units in the present area will be collected together and handed over to the respective Area Commandants from whom receipts and certificates that Camps and Billets have been left in a satisfactory condition will be obtained.
Report of Locations.	12.	Detailed Location lists will be forwarded to Brigade Headquarters as early as possible after arrival in the new Area.
	13.	ACKNOWLEDGE.

J.S. Fox Captain.
Staff Captain.
199th Infantry Brigade.

B.H.Q.
14th Feb. 1918.

TABLE A.

:- SUPPLY ARRANGEMENTS DURING MOVE :-

Serial No.	Units travelling by train No.	Group.	Rations Date Drawn	Rations For Consumption	Remarks.
1.	Part P.2.3.4. 5.6.7.8.	199th Inf. Bde.	16	17	Railhead by Train transport. By units' 1st line transport.
2.	as above	-do-	16	18	Loaded on Train Coys. wagons which will proceed to and ontrain with Units.
3.	as above	-do-	16	20	Loaded on lorries and delivered by Train Coy. on 19th.
4.	as above	-do-	18	19	Drawn from new Railhead by Train Coy. & delivered to units.
5.	as above	-do-	19	21	Drawn by lorry from R.H. and drawn from Refilling Point on 20th by 1st Line transport. Similarly on subsequent days.

P.T.O.

LORRIES :-

1. All lorries to report at Brigade Headquarters, SCHOUL Camp, L.5.d.8.C., (sheet 27), at 4.0 p.m., February 16th, are allotted as under :-

	No. of lorries.
Brigade Headquarters	2
Battalions (at 2 each)	6
Machine Gun Company	1
Trench Mortar Battery	1
Field Ambulance	1
	11

2. Units are responsible that the following instructions are strictly adhered to :-

   (a) No lorry will make more than one journey to station of entrainment, except in case of a breakdown.

   (b) After off-loading, all lorries will return at once to destination as ordered by their own M.T. unit.

   (c) An Officer, and unloading party (strength not less than 1 N.C.O. and 4 men per lorry) will accompany each lorry or group of lorries. This Officer must have written instructions.

   (d) Lorries must be off-loaded as quickly as possible.

   (e) All lorries must arrive at entraining station 3 hours before times of departure of trains as laid down in this office A.899 of 13.2.18.

   (f) All baggage belonging to an Infantry or Pioneer Battalion will be loaded on to the train which carries its Headquarters.

   (g) Lorries will as far as possible be detailed by the D.A.A.G., 66th Division to meet train at the detraining station in accordance with above allotment.

SECRET.   Copy No. 9

199th Infantry Brigade
WARNING ORDER.

Ref: Maps - Sheets 62^d, 62^c, and 62^b. 1/40,000.

MOVE AND RELIEF. 1. (a) The 66th Division accompanied by Divnl. Supply Column and Ammunition Sub-Park, will be transferred from XIX Corps to Cavalry Corps between the 24th February and 3rd March, and will relieve the 24th Division in the line.

(b) The 199th Inf.Bde. will move from HARBONNIERES to VILLERS - CARBONNEL on February 24th, thence to ERNES - HANCOURT area on February 25th, thence to line (Right) on February 26th, and night of 26/27th in relief of 72nd Infantry Brigade.

DISPOSITION. 2. On completion of relief the 199th Infantry Brigade will be disposed as follows :-

  2/5th Lanch.Regt. in Front Line (just west of GRAND PRIEL WOOD, approximately).

  2/6th   "   "   Support.

  2/7th   "   "   Reserve - hutted camp at HERZILLY.

  Bde. H.Q.   at HAUT WOODS (L.7.c.).

MARCH. 3. Orders for marches will be issued later.

4. ACKNOWLEDGE.

                                              Captain,
                                              Brigade Major,
20.2.18.   199th Infantry Brigade.

Distribution:-

Copy No. 1.....G.O.C.
 "   "   2.....Brigade Major.
 "   "   3.....Staff Captain.
 "   "   4.....Bde.Sigs.Officer.
 "   "   5.....2/5th Lanch.Regt.
 "   "   6.....2/6th   "   "
 "   "   7.....2/7th   "   "
 "   "   8.....204th M.G.Coy.
 "   "   9.....199th L.T.M.B.
 "   " 10.....2/3rd Fld.Amb.
 "   " 11.....432nd Fld.Coy.R.E.
 "   " 12.....544 Coy.A.S.C.
 "   " 13.....War Diary.
 "   " 14.....
 "   " 15.....File.
 "   " 16.....Spare.
 "   " 17.....   "

SECRET.   Copy No. 9

199th Infantry Brigade.
OPERATION ORDER No. 81

Ref Maps ROSIERES (combined sheet) } 1/40,000.
          Sheet 62 c

Move. 1. The 199th Infantry Brigade will move into the Cavalry Corps Area, and relieve 72nd Brigade, 24th Division as follows.

(a) On Feb 24th by march route from HARBONNIERES SUB-AREA to staging camp about 1½ miles west of VILLERS CARBONNEL.

(b) On Feb 25th by march route from VILLERS CARBONNEL to BERNES - HANCOURT AREA.

(c) On Feb 26th from BERNES - HANCOURT AREA to Line (Right).

March Details
2. (a) March Table A is attached.

(b) March Table B will be issued shortly.

(c) Orders for move and relief on Feb 26th will be issued separately.

Intervals. 3. Intervals to be maintained on the march will be the same as laid down in Fourth Army G.S. 148 for Fourth Army Area.

Lewis Guns. 4. Attention is directed to 66th Division 527/3 G of 10.2.18, forwarded under this office number G.639 of 11.2.18.

Billeting Parties. 5. 1 officer and 4 N.C.O's per unit will proceed to the first staging area in advance on 24th on cycles. This same party will proceed next day to BERNES to take up billets in 2nd staging area.

Arrangements will be made for Transport officer or Q.M. to proceed up the line to visit the transport of the units they are relieving.

6. ACKNOWLEDGE.

                                                    Captain.
                                                Brigade Major.
                                            199th Infantry Brigade.

Distribution :-
  Copy No. 1 .... G.O.C.
          2 .... Brigade Major.
          3 .... Staff Captain.
          4 .... Bde. Signal Officer.
          5 .... 2/5th Manch Regt.
          6 .... 2/6th   "   "
          7 .... 2/7th   "   "
          8 .... 204th M.G.C.
          9 .... 199th L.T.M.B.
         10 .... 2/6th M.R. Transport Offr.
         11 .... 198th Inf. Bde.
         12 .... 432nd Fd. Coy R.E.
         13 .... 544th Coy A.S.C.
         14 .... 2/3rd Fd. Ambulance.
         15 .... 66th Division "G"
         16 ....   "   "   "Q"
         17 .... War Diary.
         18 ....   "   "
         19 .... File.
         20 .... Spare.
         21 ....   "

Table "A" to accompany 199th Infantry Brigade Order No. 81.

Serial No.	Date.	Unit.	From.	To.	Starting Pt.	Time of passing S.P.	Remarks.
1.	Feb 24th	Bde H.Q.	HARBONNIERES	Staging camp about 1½ miles West of VILLERS - CARBONNEL.	Q.30.d.9.5	8.32 a.m.	2/8 Man. transport will march with Bde H.Q. transport.
2.	"	2/5th Man.Rgt.	-do-		-do-	8.38 a.m.	
3.	"	2/6th "	-do-		-do-	9.04 a.m.	
4.	"	3/7th "	BAYONVILLERS		Q.27.c.2.3	8.32 a.m.	
5.	"	2/3rd Fd.Amb. less transport	HARBONNIERES		Q.30.d.9.5	9.40 a.m.	
6.	"	204th M.G.C.	FRAMERVILLE		R.28.c.5.3	10.30 a.m.	
7.	"	199th L.T.M.B.	VAUVILLERS		-do-	10.38 a.m.	
8.	"	432nd Fd.Coy.	-do-		-do-	10.43 a.m.	
9.	"	544th Coy ASC	BAYONVILLERS		Q.27.c.2.3	9.26 a.m.	
10.	"	Transport 2/3 Fd. Amb.	HARBONNIERES		Q.30.d.9.5	10.35 a.m.	To move out of HARBONNIERES with dismounted personnel, and wait, off the road, to join in the column in rear of 544 Coy ASC at Q.30.d.9.5

ROUTE :- FOUCAUCOURT - ESTREES.

Table "B" to accompany 199th Inf. Bde. Order No. 81.

Serial No.	Date.	Unit.	From.	To.	Starting Point.	Time.	Route.	Remarks.
1.	Feb 25th	Bde H.Q. & 2/8th L.R. Transport.	VILLERS-CARBONNEL	BERNES	X roads K.30.a.3.6	9.0 am	BRID-MONS-EN-CHAUSSEE - VRAIGNES.	On Feb 25th 204th MGC.432 Fd.Coy RE will relieve corresponding units of 72nd Inf.Bde.under orders to be issued by D.A.G.,C.R.E., respectively. These units will move independently from VRAIGNES.
2.	"	2/4th Man.Rgt.	-do-	"	-do-	9.6 am		
3.	"	2/5th " "	-do-	HANCOURT A Camp.	-do-	9.24am		
4.	"	2/7th " "	-do-	"	-do-	9.42am		
5.	"	204th M.G.C.	-do-	VRAIGNES	-do-	10.0 am		
6.	"	199th L.T.M.B.	-do-	"	-do-	10.07am		
7.	"	432nd Fd. Coy.	-do-	will not move	-do-	10.11am		
8.	"	2/1st Fd. Amb.*	-do-	VRAIGNES				
9.	"	544th Coy.ASC	-do-		-do-	10.18am		

* 2/1st Field Ambulance will remain at VILLERS CARBONNEL on Feb 25th. and will move independently to DOINGT on Feb 26th.

SECRET.

AMENDMENT TO 199th INFANTRY BRIGADE ORDER No. 81.

Reference 199th Infantry Brigade Order No. 5, the following amendments will be made.

1. Para 1 (c), before " on Feb 26th" add 199th Infantry Brigade Group (less Brigade H.Q. and 2/7th Manchester Regt).

2. Add para 1 (d) "on Feb 27th Brigade H.Q. and 2/7th Manchester Regt to Line (Right)."

3. Table A. serial No. 1 delete remarks column.

4. Table A cancel serial No. 10, and add :-

   Serial No. 11 :-
   Feb 24th. 2/1st Fd. Ambulance. From WEINCOURT to VILLERS - CARBONNEL stageing area. Route BAYONVILLERS - X roads Q.27.c.2.3. Starting point Q.27.c.2.3. Time 9.33 a.m. To follow 544 Coy A.S.C. from BAYONVILLERS.

5. Serial No. 5, delete "2/3rd Fd. Ambulance leg transport" and substitute "transport 2/8th M.R."

6. 199th Brigade H.Q. will close at HARBONNIERES at 7.0 a.m. on February 24th.

ACKNWLEDGE.

23.2.18.

Captain.
Brigade Major.
199th Infantry Brigade.

To all recipients of 199th Infantry Brigade Order No.81.
Copy to 2/1st Field Ambulance.

SECRET.   Copy No. 9

199th Infantry Brigade.
OPERATION ORDER No. 82.

Ref Maps.   Sheet 62 c 1/40,000
             HARGICOURT 1/10,000 Trench map.

Relief. 1. (a) The 199th Infantry Brigade Group (less 2/3rd Field Ambulance) will relieve the 72nd Infantry Brigade Group in Right Subsector of VILLERET SECTOR on Feb. 26th and 27th.
(b) Reliefs will take place in accordance with attached Table "A".

Taking over. 2. All trench maps, trench stores, aeroplane photographs, defence schemes etc., will be taken over, and receipts given. Copies of receipts to be forwarded to Bde. H.Q.

Working Parties. 3. (a) Details of working parties required by R.E. and Division will be issued later.
(b) Details of work in progress in the line will be taken over, and the work carried on.

Advance Parties. 4. There will be 3 lorries at ABADIE CIRCUS N.27.d.7.5 at 9.0 a.m. on Feb 25th, to take advance parties to the forward area. Following advance parties (exclusive of those detailed in Administrative Orders) will be sent:-
H.Q., Front Line and Support Battalion. 1 officer per Bn./and 1 officer and 4 N.C.O's per Company.
Front Line Battalion. 1 Patrol Officer per front line Company.
Reserve Battalion. 1 officer, 4 N.C.O's.
204th M.G.Coy. 1 officer and 4 N.C.O's.
199th L.T.M.B. 1 Officer

Completion 5. Completion of relief will be reported by code number 50.

Bde. H.Q. 6. Brigade H.Q. will close on Feb. 27th at BYRNES at a time to be notified later, and will reopen at K.29.b.75.70 on completion of relief, when command will pass to G.O.C. 199th Infantry Brigade.

7. ACKNOWLEDGE.

R. Brodie
Captain.
Brigade Major.
199th Infantry Brigade.

B.H.Q.
23rd Feb. 1918.

Distribution :-

Copy No.			Copy No.	
1	......	G.O.C.	12	.... 452nd Fd. Coy. R.E.
2	......	Brigade Major.	13	.... 544th Coy A.S.C.
3	......	Staff Captain.	14	.... 2/1st Fd.Amb.
4	......	Bde.Sig.Offr.	15	.... 66th Div. "G"
5	......	2/5th M.Rgt.	16	.... " " "Q"
6	......	2/5th "	17	.... War Diary.
7	......	2/7th " "	18	.... " "
8	......	204th M.G.C.	19	.... File.
9	......	199th L.T.M.B.	20	.... Spare.
10	......	2/8th M.R.Transport Officer.	21	.... "
			22	.... 72nd Inf. Bde.
11	......	198th Inf.Bde.	23	.... 2/3rd Fd. Amb.

Table "A" to accompany 199th Infantry Brigade Order No. 82.

Serial No.	Date.	Unit.	From.	To.	Relieves.	Remarks.
1	Feb 26th	2/5th K.R.	HARCOURT.	Line H.Q. THE EGG L.17.b.5.5	9th E.Surrey R.	From HARCOURT by Light Railway. 2 Coys (Right and Left Front) leave HARCOURT 11.0 a.m. arrive TEMPLEUX 1.0 p.m., where guides 1 per Bn. H.Q. & 1 per platoon will meet. Bn. H.Q. & 2 Coys (Line Centre & Support) leave HARCOURT 2.30 p.m. arrive TEMPLEUX 4.30 p.m. guides as above. See also Serial No. 4.
2.	"	2/5th K.R.	BERNES.	Support. H.Q.L.10.c.7.4	1st Bn.N.Staffs Regt.	By Light Railway. Leave BERNES about 11.50 a.m. arrive TEMPLEUX at 2.0 p.m. guides as above.
3.	"	204th MGC	VRAIGNES	H.Q. COTE WOOD	72nd M.G.Coy.	Orders to be issued later by D.M.G.C.
4.	"	199th LT.M.B	"	Line	72nd L.T.M.B.	Details to be arranged by O.Cs. L.T.M.B. moves to TEMPLEUX by 1st train of serial No. 1 above.
5.	"	2/1st Fd.Am.	VILLERS – DOINGT. CARBONNEL	—	—	Moves independently. Details of relief arranged by A.D.M.S. and O.C. 2/1st Fd.Amb.
6.	"	544th Coy. A.S.C.	VRAIGNES	—	—	Does not move.
7.	Feb 27th	Bde H.Q.	BERNES	E.29.b.75.70	72nd Bde H.Q.	By march route.
8.	"	2/4th R.R.	HARCOURT	VILLELLES	8th Royal W. Kents.	By march route. Time to be notified later.

NOTE :- Times of Light railway trains are subject to confirmation by 24th : Div "Q". Exact entraining places will be notified later.

SECRET.   Copy No. 9

199th Infantry Brigade
ADMINISTRATIVE ORDER No. 38.

Move of 199th Infantry Brigade Group (less 2/3rd Fld Amb.)
from BERNES AREA to the Line.

ADVANCE TRANSPORT PARTIES.	will meet the B.T.O. at ABADIE CIRCUS, N.27.d.7.5
Bde. H.Q. 1 Offr.	on 25th inst at 9.0 a.m. and will proceed to
2/5 M.R.- 9th E.Surreys	72nd Bde. H.Q. They will be sent to the units
- 1 Offr.	they are relieving and will proceed with the
2/6 M.R.- 1st N.Staffs	transport taking rations up 25th/26th inst.
- 1 Offr.	This party will join their units at MONTIGNY
2/7 M.R.- 8th Royal W.	on the 26th inst.
Kents - 1 Offr.	
204 MGC - 72 MGC-1 Offr.	
199 LTMB- 72 LTMB-1Offr.	

TRANSPORT LINES.   will be at MONTIGNY for the following :-

        199th Bde. H.Q.
        2/5th Lan.Rgt.
        2/6th   "   "
        2/7th   "   "
        204th M.G.Coy.
        432nd Fd.Coy.R.E.

S.A.A. & GRENADE STORE, & GUM BOOT STORES.   These are at Battalion H.Q's and are under charge of units who will provide necessary caretakers.
Reports as to amount of S.A.A. and Grenades and Gum Boots taken over will be sent to this office on the 1st Prox.

LORRIES.   Lorries will be allotted as under :-

2 each Battalion, 1 L.T.M.B., 1 M.G.Coy., and 1 432nd Fd. Coy. R.E.

Guides for lorries will report at Staff Captain's office, HARBONNIERES at 8.0 a.m. on the 24th inst.
Lorries will remain with units until completion of move.
An officer will accompany each lorry or convoy.

SUPPLIES.   Supply arrangements during move are shown on attached Table "A".

R.E.MATERIAL.   There are R.E. Dumps at each Battalion H.Q's.
Main Dump situated at MONTIGNY.

RESERVE RATIONS.   Great care will be taken in taking over Reserve Rations. These will be checked and receipts given for exact amounts, and locations of rations and quantities will be forwarded to this office by the 1st prox.

MEDICAL.   2/1st Field Ambulance will attend to sick of this Brigade until the 27th inst, when the 74th Field Ambulance will take over the sick until arrival of 2/3rd Field Ambulance.

                                                    J.S.Fox Captain.
                                                  Staff Captain.
23.2.18.   199th Infantry Brigade.

                                                                                 P.T.O.

DISTRIBUTION

```
Copy No. 1 ..... G.O.C.
"    "   2 ..... Brigade Major.
"    "   3 ..... Staff Captain.
"    "   4 ..... Bde. Sigs. Officer.
"    "   5 ..... 2/5th Manch. Regt.
"    "   6 ..... 2/6th   "     "
"    "   7 ..... 2/7th   "     "
"    "   8 ..... 204th M.G.Coy.
"    "   9 ..... 199th L.T.M.B.
"    "  10 ..... 2/1st Field Ambulance.
"    "  11 ..... 2/3rd    "      "
"    "  12 ..... 432nd Fd. Coy. R.E.
"    "  13 ..... 544th Coy A.S.C.
"    "  14 ..... Q.M. 2/5th Manch Regt.
"    "  15 .....  "   2/6th  "     "
"    "  16 .....  "   2/7th  "     "
"    "  17 ..... Transport Officer 2/8th M.R.
"    "  18 ..... 72nd Inf. Bde.
"    "  19 ..... Area Comdt. HARBONNIERES.
"    "  20 ..... 63th Div. "BQ"
"    "  21 ..... War Diary.
"    "  22 .....   "    "
"    "  23 ..... File.
"    "  24 ..... Spare.
"    "  25 .....   "
```

Table "A" to accompany 199th Infantry Brigade Administrative Order No. 38.

Serial No.	Group.	Rations for Consumption.	Drawn at Railhead by.	Delivered to Units by.	Remarks.
1	199 Bde. Group (with 2/1 Fld.Amb. instead of 2/3rd)	25th	Div.Train on 23rd	Train transport on 24th at VILLERS CARBONNEL Staging Camp.	
2.	ditto	26th	Div.Supply Column on 24th	Train Transport on 25th at HARCOURT area.	
3.	ditto	27th	Div.Supply Column on 25th	Train transport on 26th at Bde.Transport Lines.	
4.	ditto	28th (and after)	Light Railways on 25th at ROISEL (off 24th Div.Park.)	1st line transport on 27th	199 Bde Group Refilling Point on light Railway at K.36.a.4.2.

66th Div.
No. 5054/Q.

SECRET.

O.C.,
2/5th [Manchester Regt.]
2/6th [...]
2/7th [...]
[...] [Machine Gun Coy.]
199th T.M. Battery
2/1st Field Ambulance.
[...]
2/4th E. Lanch. Regt. (Pioneers).

H.Q.,
199TH INFANTRY BDE.
No. A.Q.21
Date...........

ADMINISTRATIVE ORDER No. [...]

The following Administrative Instructions are issued in continuation of 199th Inf. Bde. Administration Order No. [..] of 22.2.16.

STARTING & STABLING.
Units will ensure that all staging areas are left in as clean and sanitary a condition as possible, and that adequate rear parties including officers, are left behind after the main column has moved off.

On arrival in the BERNES - HANCOURT - VRAIGNES area, units will be disposed as follows :-

2/5th in A Camp

Brigade Headquarters and 2/6th Manch.R. in BERNES.
~~2/5~~ 2/7th Manch. Regt. in HANCOURT. ~~Artillery~~
Field Company, Field Ambulance, Company of the Train, Machine Gun Company and Trench Mortar Battery at VRAIGNES.
Cyclist advanced parties will report in advance to the Area Commandant's at VRAIGNES (for VRAIGNES and HANCOURT) and BERNES.
All units in each Brigade Group, and their transport must be clear of the BERNES - HANCOURT - VRAIGNES area 48 hours after arrival.
The final distribution of units in the new Divisional area will be as shown in Table B - (to be forwarded later).

ORDNANCE ARRANGEMENTS.
The Divisional Ordnance Store at VILLERS - BRETONNEUX will close at 4.0 p.m. on the 27th instant, and open at G.X.B., one mile North of HANCOURT on March 1st.

MEDICAL ARRANGEMENTS.
The day after arrival in the HANCOURT - VRAIGNES area, the Field Ambulances will relieve corresponding units of the 24th Division as follows :-
2/1st Field Ambulance relieves 72nd Field Ambulance at the Divisional Rest Station DOINGT on the 28th February.
2/2nd Field Ambulance relieves 74th Field Ambulance at ROISEL on 28th February.
2/3rd Field Ambulance relieves 73rd Field Ambulance at the Main Dressing Station, BERNES, and takes over the evacuation system in the forward zone on March 2nd.
Advanced Dressing Stations are situated as follows :-
HESPLINE LE SUBBARD,   L.2.c.9.8.
ROISEL,   K.14.d.8.2.
BUSSECOURT Road,   K.12.d.5.2. - now under construction.

The A.D.M.S. will arrange to issue to medical officers of all units prior to relief in the line detailed instructions as to the method of evacuation from the R.A.P.

P.T.O.

(2).

VETERINARY. On arrival in the new area on March 3rd, the Mobile Veterinary Section will take over the lines of the 24th Division Mobile Veterinary Section at VRAIGNES.
Evacuation takes place by rail from ROISEL on Tuesdays and Fridays to No. 7 Veterinary Hospital, FORGES LES EAUX.

REINFORCE-MENT WING. The Divisional Reinforcement Camp Staff will move by lorry with Divisional Headquarters on March 3rd from VILLERS-CARBONNEL to HANCOURT, where the Reinforcement Wing (as well as a Divisional School for officers) will open shortly.

Administrative instructions with reference to salvage, canteens, baths, recreation rooms, etc. will be issued later.

B.H.Q.
24.2.18.

Captain,
Staff Captain,
199th Infantry Brigade.

SUMMARY FOR MONTH

Army Form C. 2118.

WAR DIARY
or
INTELLIGENCE SUMMARY.
(Erase heading not required.)

Place	Date	Hour	Summary of Events and Information	Remarks and references to Appendices
R sub sec (D) Villeneuvettes, part of Villeneuvettes L.T.M.B.			During the month of February the 199th L.T.M.B. was relieved in the line (Zonnebeke Sector) by the 94th & and 161st L.T.M.Bs. (Feb 9th) and left (Feb 17th) a few days at School Camp near Proven, entrained (Feb 17th) at Proven and arrived at Vauvillers on Feb 18th. After resting at Vauvillers for a few days the Battery proceeded to the line (Feb 24th, 25th, 26th) and relieved the 72nd L.T.M.B5. in the right sector of St Quentin. A.J. Smith Lt. T.M.C. (?) 199 L.T.M.B.	

TACTICAL PROGRESS REPORTS

Daily Tactical Progress Report

Unit. "COD"

From 6am 31.1.18 to 6am. 1.2.'18.

A. Operations

Our L.T.M's were inactive.

[signature] Capt.
O.C.
"COD"

Daily Tactical Progress Report

Unit:- "COD"
From 6am 1.2.18 to 6am 2.2.18

A Operations

Our L.T.M's were inactive.

[signature]
Capt.
O.C.
"COD"

Daily Tactical Progress Report

Unit:- "C.O.D"
From 6am 2.2.18 to 6am 3.2.18

A) Operations:

Our L.T.M's were inactive

[signature]
Capt.
O.C
"COD"

Daily Tactical Progress Report

Unit:- "C" Coy
From 6am 3.2.18 to 6am 4.2.18.

A Operations

Our L.T.M's were inactive.

[signature]
Capt
o.c
"C" Coy

Daily Tactical Progress Report

Unit:- "C O I"

From 6am 4.2.18 to 6am 5.2.18

A. Operations

Our L.T.M's were inactive

[signature]
Capt
o.c.
"C O I"

Daily Tactical Progress Report

Unit:- "C O D"

From 6am 5.2.18 to 6am 6.2.18

A Operations

Our L T M's were inactive.

[signature]

Capt
OC
"COD"

Daily Tactical Progress Report

Unit:- "C O D"

From 6am 6.2.18 to 6am 7.2.18

A Operations

L.T.M's. were inactive.

[signature]
Capt.
O.C.
"COD".

Daily Tactical Progress Report

Unit:- "C O I"

From 6am 7.2.18 to 6am 8.2.18

A Operations

At 7.15pm my gun at D.11.d.88.50 fired a salvo of 10 shells at the enemy M.G. at TIBER COPSE which, since dusk, had been very active. Infantry in front line posts report that the shells all fell on the mark (D.12.a.20.40. app) and that this M.G was silent during the remainder of the night.

[signature]
Capt.
OC
"COI"

N.B. Infantry report that lights were seen in the vicinity of where the shells fell immediately after the shoot.

Daily Tactical Progress Report

Unit:- C Coy

From 6am 8.2.18 to 6am 9.2.18

A Operations:

Stokes at D.11.d.88.80 fired two bursts of 5 rounds into TIBER COPSE during the night.

Stokes at D.18.a.40.70 shelled suspected enemy post at D.18.b.30.70 with 10 rounds at 7 p.m.

Kenneth Mailey
Capt
o/c
"C Coy"

Daily Tactical Progress Report

Unit. 20D.

From 6 am 27.2.18 to 6 am. 28.2.'18.

A) Operations.

At 8.30 am, our two guns at G.7.d.8.8 and G.7.d.9.3 respectively fired in retaliation to enemy T.M. at G.8.c.7.3. During the afternoon this target was again engaged. At 3 pm our gun at G.7.d.8.8. fired on enemy rifle grenade post about G.8.a.8.0. approximately.

a J Luff/b
Lieut
O.C.
20D

Daily Tactical Progress Report

Unit:- C.O.D

From 6am 26.2.18 to 6am 27.2.18

A. **Operations**

Owing to relief our L.T.M's were inactive. At about midnight the S.O.S. was sent up but it was at once seen the disturbance was out of range of our guns and they remained silent.

A. J. Smith.
Lieut
O.C.
C.O.D

www.ingramcontent.com/pod-product-compliance
Lightning Source LLC
Chambersburg PA
CBHW080914230426
43667CB00015B/2675